Louisa May Alcott

a reference guide

A
Reference
Publication
in
Literature

Jack Salzman
Editor

Louisa May Alcott

a reference guide

ALMA J. PAYNE

G.K.HALL&CO.

70 LINCOLN STREET, BOSTON, MASS.

Library of Congress Cataloging in Publication Data

Payne, Alma J
  Louisa May Alcott, a reference guide.

  (Reference guide in literature)
  Includes index.
  1. Alcott, Louisa May, 1832-1888—Bibliography.
I. Title. II. Series.
Z8024.8.P39   [PS1018]   016.813'4   79-23374
ISBN 0-8161-8032-6

This publication is printed on permanent/durable acid-free paper
MANUFACTURED IN THE UNITED STATES OF AMERICA

For Lyon N. Richardson,
Mentor and Dear Friend

Contents

Introduction

Although the work of the bibliographer may be regarded by some as
necessary "busy work," the literary-cultural historian finds the survey of critical treatment of an author and of the author's work to be
revealing and rewarding. If the writer is complex and many-faceted,
the mosaic of criticism presents pictures of societal as well as literary attitudes and values. Although generally regarded during much
of the present century as the author of one book, <u>Little Women</u>,
Louisa May Alcott has emerged as just such a many-faceted personality,
appealing in turn to the variant literary, social, and cultural em-
phases of a changing America.

Alcott may be viewed as a true daughter of Concord, dutiful child
of the high priest of transcendentalism, Amos Bronson Alcott; a young
companion of Thoreau; and the devoted disciple of Emerson. As a literary figure, she can be studied as a direct product of the newly
emergent periodical, beginning as pseudonymous author of lurid and
sentimental Gothic "pot-boilers," realistically recording her service
as a Civil War nurse, and emerging as the world renowned author of
accounts of American family life which have assumed the stature of
myth. With the raising of feminine consciousness Alcott is increasingly seen, not as occupying the pedestal bestowed by the Cult of
True Womanhood, but as a professional woman, serving as an important
role model for young women and joining actively in the advocacy of
abolition, woman suffrage, and educational, labor, and prison reform.

There can be no denial of the importance of Concord and New England as factors contributing to the character, the values, and the
subject matter of Louisa May Alcott. Her family was the center of
her life in many ways, for she was taught by her father under his
advanced educational theories. Her friends included Emerson, Thoreau,
the Hawthornes, and those befriended by her philanthropic parents,
who shared their few means with escaping slaves, John Brown's family,
and many victims of the new industrialization. Poverty and uncer-
tainty marked her early years and enforced her determination to "provide" for her family. On the other hand, the books and dramas which
she read gave her an awareness of the melodramatic and sensational as
well as of the drama of the realistic "pilgrim's progress" of

everyday life. All that she did, all that she experienced, teaching, sewing, going out to service, acting as a companion, provided the raw materials for her literary creations.

Alcott had many audiences for these works. Her first published book, Flower Fables (1855), introduces the charming, imaginative fantasies which appealed to young children. Dedicated to Ellen Emerson, daughter of Alcott's friend Ralph Waldo Emerson, it combined colorful prose and delicate poetry, peopling the child's world with fairies, elves, and the small animals to which Louisa had been introduced by Thoreau. The simple stories and songs taught patience, duty, honor and, above all, the power of love. The influence of Transcendentalism is evident in the importance discovered in all living things, but the enchanted world which Alcott created sufficed for the child audience. Alcott never forgot this audience during her thirty years of creative production; even in her last years, Alcott revived her fairy world for the little niece entrusted to her care upon the death of her sister May.

In 1943 with the publication of Leona Rostenberg's "Some Anonymous and Pseudonymous Thrillers of Louisa May Alcott," Alcott's modern public became aware of her many pieces of sensational fiction, aimed at an avid periodical audience. Appearing in Frank Leslie's Illustrated Newspaper, The Flag of Our Union, and other periodicals, under various pseudonyms such as "Flora Fairfield," "A. M.," and "A. M. Barnard," these stories relieved the family financial distress and provided an excellent apprenticeship for Alcott, who frankly enjoyed producing the "gorgeous and lurid." When examined in contrast to others of the genre, these stories demonstrate her developing control of characterization and timing and provide interesting "seeds" of later, better-known works.

In the opinion of Madeleine Stern, Alcott could have achieved a successful and lucrative, if not long-lived, career in the pages of the Saturday Evening Gazette and Frank Leslie's Illustrated Newspaper. However, Louisa's duty to a larger family than her own led to her experience as Civil War nurse and the resulting Hospital Sketches (1863), revealing real-life drama more impressive than any Gothic in its horror and in its revelation of human dignity. It is not an exaggeration to state that the experiences of Alcott's persona, "Tribulation Periwinkle," not only reflect the realities of the author's nursing career but also rank with Whitman's poetic record in the depiction of suffering, gallantly borne, the humor present even in such trials, and the compassion of those serving as nurses. The favorable critical reception accorded the book must have convinced Alcott that success might lie in portraying real life rather than realms of fancy.

In 1868 Louisa May Alcott established the reading audience which continues today when Little Women, 1 received universal critical approval. Little Women, 2 followed in 1869 and success was complete, largely because, as Alcott said of the novel, "We really lived most of it." Using this experience as her starting point, she created characters which entered American literature. <u>Little Women</u> (1868-1869) was followed by seven others: <u>An Old-Fashioned Girl</u> (1870), <u>Little Men</u> (1871), <u>Eight Cousins</u> (1875), <u>Rose in Bloom</u> (1876), <u>Under the Lilacs</u> (1878), <u>Jack and Jill</u> (1880), and <u>Jo's Boys</u> (1886).

Before the last of the series appeared, Alcott had become a literary institution and a role model for the emerging "New Woman" who sought to climb down from the pedestal of "True Womanhood" and achieve fulfillment and sexual independence. In the <u>Little Women</u> series she commented on familial roles, on values, customs, and dress of Victorian society; especially in <u>Little Men</u> and <u>Jo's Boys</u> she personified the avant-garde educational philosophy of Amos Bronson Alcott and critically examined the impact of urban environment and social Darwinism.

Although the knowledge of the majority of her readers is limited to the works described above, an examination of the almost three hundred items in Alcott's canon reveals that she wrote on many contemporary problems in both fiction and non-fiction. From childhood she was involved in the cause of freedom for American blacks. She supported prison reform and opposed child labor. As befitted the creator of Jo March, Alcott was a powerful advocate of woman suffrage, and, until her death in 1888, used the power of her person and her pen to demonstrate her loyalty and her determination never to desert "her flag."

As a consequence of the many levels on which Louisa May Alcott wrote, of the many audiences to which she appealed, and of the many problems and values of American society which she addressed, the critical reactions to Alcott have been variant.

The criticism written within her lifetime was obviously shaped by Alcott's growing success. While <u>Flower Fables</u> was sponsored by Mrs. Hawthorne and praised by Alcott's father and his friends as recorded in his <u>Journal</u> for 17 November 1854, its publisher, Fields, advised her "to stick to her teaching." The thirty-two dollars which she received, however, encouraged her to submit more and more pseudonymous tales and there was soon a demand for stories by "Flora Fairfield," "A. M.," "A. M. Barnard," and "L. M. A." Despite careful searching I have been unable to find critical comments, other than publishers' "blurbs," dealing with these early pseudonymous "pot-boilers."

Only after Louisa had undergone the trial by fire of her nursing experience did the first recognition of her ability to create, as shown in <u>Hospital Sketches</u> with its persona of "Tribulation Periwinkle," begin to appear. Henry James expressed his pleasure in "Louisa's Sketches" in a letter to her father and sent her a copy of his <u>Substance and Shadow</u>. In subsequent entries in his <u>Journal</u> for

1863, Amos Bronson Alcott recorded the "good appreciation of Louisa's merits as a woman and a writer" and his amazement at the admiration expressed by publishers like Redpath and Fields and in the Boston Transcript, Waterbury American, the Liberator and elsewhere.

The favorable reception of Hospital Sketches encouraged Alcott to revise and publish Moods, upon which she had been working since 1860. Despite her father's praise for her "treatment of the social problem" and her "vigorous and clear" style along with her forceful characterization, the critical reception was indifferent and Louisa vowed to abandon idea for facts, to make "the people . . . as ordinary as possible; then critics will say it's all right" (Journals [5 April 1865], 166). Henry James's comments in North American Review [1865.3] questioned her knowledge of human nature and he gave prophetically good advice when he urged her to employ her excellent style "to describe only that which she has seen" and thus produce "a novel above the average."

Almost against her will, Alcott produced such a novel four years later. Little Women received instantaneous praise throughout the United States and abroad. The happy marriage of clear style, resulting from her periodical apprenticeship, and the raw material of the life she and her family had lived resulted in a book which appealed to all ages in all places. Written in two parts, Little Women (1868) and Good Wives (1869), the novel established Alcott's success. Typical of the critical reviews were those in the Nation which saw the book as "not only very well adapted to the readers for whom it is especially intended, but [it] may also be read with pleasure by older people" [1868.6]. Some critics regarded Little Women as "rather mature" for its audience [1869.2]. The Nation recognized the close parallel between "Jo" and Alcott and warned that the book's great success might inhibit "the author's pretensions to do better work in the future" [1869.3].

An Old-Fashioned Girl surpassed Little Women in sales, if not in excellence, selling 12,000 copies in advance and 27,000 in the first month after publication [A. B. Alcott, Journals (1 April, 2 May 1870)]. Harper's judged it to be more popular than Little Women with an older audience but wondered whether it threatened "the tyrranical reign of Mrs. Grundy" [1870.6]. Lippincott's praised it for its "delicate and faithful portraiture" and "simple, graceful, and modest style" [1870.7]. Only the minority voice of The Atlantic Monthly criticized the bad grammar and poor writing [1870.2].

The appearance of Little Men in 1871 was greeted by praise for the skill of Alcott in picturing a child world but by more doubts as to the book's artistic merit. Godey's Lady's Book compared Alcott to Edgeworth as "the children's author" [1871.2], but Harper's found the work to be lacking in plot and movement [1871.3]. The same periodical joined others in questioning the type of education proposed--an educational philosophy based upon the avant-garde system of her father.

Despite such doubts, there was a prepublication sale of 50,000 [A. B. Alcott, Journals, 418].

Eight Cousins received a severely critical review by Henry James, who found the book lacking in artistic style and in tone. The book was "unfortunate not only in its details but in its general tone, in the constant ring of its style." He was alarmed at the author's sympathy with the earthy attitudes, taste, and language of the children who made a habit of putting adults in their place. In Eight Cousins he found no glow, no fairies, but only "rather vulgar prose" [1875.4].

Although the remaining volumes in the Little Women series continued to be financial successes, there was little or no critical reference to artistic merits and an increasing tendency to class the author and the works as "juvenile." The Literary World saw Rose in Bloom as weakened by "the worm of sickly sentiment . . . gnawing at its heart" [1876.1]. Alcott regarded A Modern Mephistopheles (1877) as an attempt at "something graver than magazine stories or juvenile literature," but few critics recognized this volume in Roberts Brothers' No Name Series as belonging to Alcott. The Atlantic Monthly reviewer guessed that Julian Hawthorne was the author and sensed in it "a signal force of some kind . . ." [1877.1]; Edward R. Burlingame recognized it as having the "defects and merits of a woman's pen," "a fresh and dainty fantasy" although romanticized [1877.4].

Under the Lilacs and Jack and Jill were repeatedly described as "charming," "vivacious" but lacking in the character typical of Alcott. A representative reaction was expressed by The Atlantic Monthly when the reviewer queried, ". . . we object to the blood-and-thunder literature, and when in place of it we have the milk-and-sugar we object again. What do we want?" [1881.1]. With Jo's Boys in 1886, reviewers welcomed back "the bright boys and girls" of an earlier Alcott and delighted in the parallels between the writing careers of Mrs. "Jo" Bhaer and Miss Alcott. However, nothing was said of Alcott's artistry. Other works immediately preceding Alcott's death were regarded as "of little children for little children" [1886.2].

The death of Louisa May Alcott produced a flood of tributes, many nostalgic, almost all reinforcing Alcott's own diagnosis of her position when she wrote, "I asked for bread and got a stone,--in the shape of a pedestal" [Journal, June, July, August, 1875]. Ednah D. Cheney, who published Louisa May Alcott: The Children's Friend in 1888 [1888.2], followed it in 1889 with Louisa May Alcott: Her Life, Letters and Journals [1889.2]. This second work, based upon personal knowledge of, and friendship with, the Alcott family, was very valuable in preserving events and attitudes which would have been lost to another biographer at a later date. Her introduction established not only her basis for selection, sometimes referred to as bowdlerizing,

but also a critical interpretation which has assumed mythic propor-
tions. She emphasized the extremely autobiographical nature of
Alcott's "best" work, downplaying the pseudonymous tales which might
threaten the image of "Duty's Child," as Bronson Alcott had character-
ized her.

Since, as Cheney revealed, Alcott had edited many parts of her
journals and had instructed that most of her letters be destroyed,
this collection assumed even greater authority. Most reviewers
accepted Cheney's interpretation but The Atlantic Monthly saw a life
"full of contradictions," revealing a nature "with powers half understood, restlessly beating against the cage, yet showing almost a
fierce solicitude for all its similarly emprisoned companions." The
reviewer was convinced "that great possibilities were lost in Miss
Alcott's career" [1890.1]. This minority view was to be heard again
after World War I.

Other reminiscences and recollections reinforced the "myth" of
Alcott. Among them was Lurabel Harlow's Louisa May Alcott: A
Souvenir [1888.3], which stressed the struggle between "ideality"
and necessity and revealed the contemporary appreciation of Hospital
Sketches as well as the Little Women series. Throughout the 1890s
there were a number of reminiscent treatments by friends, such as
Maria S. Porter's "Recollections of Louisa May Alcott" in New England
Magazine [1892.1]. Personal details give life to the usual outline
of Alcott's early life, the struggles at Fruitlands, and Louisa's
dramatic flair. There are revelations of the satiric eye with which
Alcott regarded her father's School of Philosophy and of the very
modern feminist championship, known to her friends, but lost in the
development of "Duty's Child." In 1893 the two-volume edition of
Amos Bronson Alcott: His Life and Philosophy by Frank B. Sanborn
and W. T. Harris [1893.3] gave important insights into the father's
influence upon, and delight in, his daughter's success.

During the first decade of the new century there were few extensive
treatments. The flood of reminiscences continued with such works as
Clara Gowing's The Alcotts As I Knew Them [1909.2] and the twelve
letters from Alcott to Alfred Whitman [1901.4] which sounded the dual
notes of duty and rebellion. In Daughters of the Puritans Seth Curtis
Beach concluded that Alcott could have been a "philanthropist and
reformer," quoting her comment in 1881 when she was the first Concord
woman to vote: "I for one don't want to be ranked among idiots, fel-
ons, and minors any longer, for I am none of them" [1905.4].

This hopeful break with the "myth of Duty's Child" was not continued in the first attempt at a book-length biography, Louisa May
Alcott, Dreamer and Worker: A Story of Achievement by Belle Moses
[1909.3]. Moses did, however, supplement the Cheney Life, Letters
and Journals with comments by Alcott's contemporaries. By including
known details of publication, this work departed from the purely
reminiscent.

Introduction

In the period from 1910 to 1919 the growing interest in primary materials was indicated by Little Women Letters from the House of Alcott, collected by Jessie Bonstelle and Marion DeForest [1914.1], which provided material valuable for later biographers. A heightened awareness of the necessity to preserve primary sources was shown by the publication of Alcott Memoirs . . . from the Papers of the late Dr. Frederick L. H. Willis [1915.2]. In 1919 an attitude prophetic of the next two decades was displayed by Gamaliel Bradford who apologized for Alcott's literary worth and stressed her morality and humanitarian "preaching" [1919.3-4].

The 1920s saw predictable attacks upon "Victorian" aspects of Alcott's life and work as in Katharine F. Gerould's Modes and Morals [1920.1] and Elizabeth Vincent's "Subversive Miss Alcott" [1924.2]. It was evident that the "pedestal" which Alcott had deplored was no longer secure. The memoirs, however, continued as in Memories of Concord [1926.3] and May Alcott/A Memoir by Caroline Ticknor [1929.5]. The last year of the decade saw one of the first twentieth-century recognitions of Louisa May Alcott's abolitionism in "Louisa May Alcott's 'M. L.'" by Lorenzo Dow Turner who rediscovered the 1863 tale [1929.6].

Despite the difficulties of the depression years, the 1932 centenary celebration of Louisa May Alcott's birth was marked by increased reader interest and important publications. The first authentic bibliographical study, Lucile Gulliver's Louisa May Alcott/ A Bibliography [1932.10], annotated all known editions and featured an "appreciation" by Cornelia Meigs. The work has been of primary importance to all subsequent bibliographers.

The year 1933 saw the publication of Cornelia L. Meigs's The Story of the Author of Little Women/Invincible Louisa [1933.7], which won the Newbery Medal. Not a critical evaluation of Alcott's works, it did provide background valuable for an understanding of those works. Reviews were generally favorable, praising new materials and the image of a growing, changing Alcott who knew "the differences between 'moral pap' and the living word" [1933.2].

In 1936 Katharine S. Anthony's "The Happiest Years" in North American Review [1936.3] told of the years which Louisa called "the golden age of the Alcotts" spent at Hillside. This was the first version of a psychoanalytic study culminating in Louisa May Alcott in 1938 [1938.3]. Critics were divided, with some reacting favorably to this attempt to apply Freud to the parent-child relationship and Alcott's "psychic ills" in later years; others charged a failure to relate Alcott to her age. Marion Talbot, one of the few remaining contemporaries of Alcott, denied that a life of duty led to spiritual sterility and presented as evidence Alcott's activity in educational reform, suffrage, and labor reform [1938.13]. The "myth" was definitely weakening.

Less controversial was Odell Shepard's carefully selected one-volume selection, The Journals of Bronson Alcott [1938.10], which gave a firm scholarly basis for the assessment of the importance of the familial and literary relationship of the Alcotts, father and daughter.

Although known by contemporaries, Alcott's anonymous and pseudonymous ventures had been buried beneath the myths of Louisa May as "Duty's Child" and "Mother of Little Women." The rediscovery and expansion of this facet of the author's career belong to two women whose criticism dominated the decade of the 1940s. Leona Rostenberg's "Some Anonymous and Pseudonymous Thrillers of Louisa M. Alcott" [1943.5] provided general knowledge of the sensational stories appearing under such names as "A. M. Barnard" and "Flora Fairfield" in Frank Leslie's Illustrated Newspaper and The Flag of Our Union. Miss Rostenberg's disclosures were supplemented by a number of articles by Madeleine B. Stern who expanded on Alcott's theatrical experiences, travels, nursing experience, and years of experimentation leading to the writing of Little Women. Stern's survey of "Louisa M. Alcott's Contributions to Periodicals, 1868-1888" [1943.8] opened a new and popular area for scholarship and enlarged the scope of known Alcott work.

The decade was marked by the disclosure of two other unexplored or forgotten aspects of the enlarging Alcott canon. Sandford Salyer published Marmee/The Mother of Little Women [1949.3], making use of previously unpublished materials to demonstrate the influence of Mrs. Alcott upon the life and career of her daughter. A major interest of the 1960s was prophesied in Julia W. Harden's "Louisa Alcott's Contribution to Democracy" [1942.2], which demonstrated the influence of Garrison, Thoreau, Emerson, Bronson Alcott, and John Brown in shaping Alcott's lifelong support of the rights of American blacks.

Interest in Alcott was increasingly evident in the 1950s. There were four biographies, each with a different emphasis. Madeleine B. Stern climaxed her studies with Louisa May Alcott [1950.3], which provided a carefully researched biography plus valuable bibliography and notes. In Louisa May Alcott/Her Life [1954.4], Catherine O. Peare used many homely details of Alcott's life to appeal to young readers. Helen Waite Papashvily examined Alcott's heroines of the better-known works in All the Happy Endings [1956.1]. Critical controversy was aroused by Marjorie Worthington's Miss Alcott of Concord/A Biography [1958.12]. Most valuable here was new manuscript material, while critics resented the insertion of Worthington's own experiences and the reworking of Cheney's pioneer work.

Of great scholarly value were the bibliographical contributions of the decade. Elizabeth B. Schlesinger's "The Alcotts through Thirty Years" [1957.7] discovered thirty years of correspondence between the Alcott girls and Alfred Whitman, once a student in Concord and a familiar in the household, afterward living in Lawrence, Kansas.

Waller Barrett [1957.2] provided a valuable map of those letters and
journal passages which led to the family chronicle, Little Women.
The most scholarly contribution of the 1950s was Jacob N. Blanck's
"Louisa May Alcott" in his Bibliography of American Literature
[1955.1]. The first editions and variants of Alcott's work are
arranged chronologically, with other works arranged under three
headings: (1) biographical, bibliographical, and critical works;
(2) titles containing material by Alcott reprinted from earlier
books; and (3) dramatizations of Alcott stories.

The decade of the 1960s saw a heightened and quickened scholarly
interest, for 1968 marked the centennial of the publication of Little
Women. In 1964 a lively debate was aroused by Brigid Brophy's "Sentimentality and Louisa M. Alcott" [1964.2] which seemed at first a
violent attack upon Little Women. Calling it a "dreadful book" which
appeals to the "lowbrow," the critic goes on to explore Alcott's
"craftsmanship in sentimentality," thus once more attempting to under-
stand the continued appeal of the one-hundred-year-old work.

Helen Waite Papashvily expanded her earlier study of Alcott's
heroines into a biographical treatment in 1965 [1965.6]. A more
important biography was the reissue in 1968 of Cornelia Meigs's
Invincible Louisa [1933.7], with a new introduction. Meigs figured
critically in several publications in 1968 including an important
introduction to the Centennial Edition of Little Women [1968.13],
the editing of Glimpses of Louisa/A Centennial Sampling of the Best
Short Stories by Louisa May Alcott [1968.12], and in the October Horn
Book, a centenary issue [1968.17].

A different point of view was provided in We Alcotts/The Story of
Louisa M. Alcott's Family As Seen through the Eyes of "Marmee,"
Mother of Little Women by Aileen Fisher and Olive Rabe [1968.4].
There were many reviews and editorial treatments during the decade
but little of note was added. The general tone seemed to be that of
renewed interest in a book with a reading public which had remained
faithful during the one hundred years since Alcott touched the universal human experience.

The decade closed with the annotated, selected bibliography,
Louisa May Alcott/A Centennial for "Little Women" [1969.5], compiled
by Judith C. Ullom and prepared by the Rare Book Division of the
Library of Congress to celebrate the centennial. Although selective,
it provides ready access to selections from prefaces and contemporary
reviews, descriptions of subsequent American and foreign editions,
and details of illustrations. This bibliography did much to restore
Alcott to esteem in the history of the domestic novel without reducing
her important position in children's literature.

The variant literary treatments of Louisa May Alcott during the
1970s have provided an index to sociocultural interests as well as
to those which are traditionally literary. A number of articles

analyzed Louisa May Alcott's participation in and literary treatments of the racial and abolition causes. Abigail Hamblen examined Alcott's dramatization of the educational concepts of her father [1971.3].

Bibliographical treatments included the updated listing in the second edition of Madeleine Stern's biography [1971.6]. The 1950 bibliography was augmented and the excellent notes were included. Alma J. Payne's in-depth bibliographical essay in <u>American Literary Realism</u> [1973.4] developed the patterns evident in critical treatments and suggested potential areas for examination. A more selective bibliography was included in Payne's "Louisa May Alcott" in <u>American Women Writers, A Critical Reference Guide</u>, Volume 1 [1979.1].

Most frequent were variations upon the "woman problem." <u>Little Women</u> was examined as a feminist tract; Alcott's non-fiction works were analyzed for "statements" on suffrage, the family, marriage and sexual roles, the professional woman, and for literary reflections of Alcott's own activities. Alma J. Payne in "Duty's Child: Louisa May Alcott" [1973.3] expanded Bronson Alcott's descriptive term to include not only familial responsibility but also other duties: to artistic integrity, to the liberated woman, and to various reforms.

The examination of familiar critical themes from psycholiterary and feminist viewpoints, typical of the 1970s, marked the latest biography, <u>Louisa May: A Modern Biography of Louisa May Alcott</u> by Martha Saxton [1977.4]. Familiar facts are treated in a lively manner but the greatest originality lies in the first chapter which serves as an excellent modern summation of patterns developed in this overview. Saxton sees Alcott as achieving fulfillment in the Gothics, which she wrote "as if it were a carnal act" thus compensating for sexual repression. <u>Little Women</u> is seen not as a masterpiece but as "a regression . . . as an artist and a woman" and a stultifying "reversion to adolescent morality." Alcott admittedly became an active, contributing member of society, but she "paid a great price in loneliness." Louisa's unverbalized antagonism to her father and resulting distrust of all men contributed to a "sullen vaporous rage" which became the "guilty center of her life." Saxton sees Alcott as eventually making an uneasy peace with herself as, ironically, she achieved the success which her father had sought in vain.

Thus, the problems of Alcott as "Duty's Child," as "New Woman," as heiress of Transcendentalism, as social critic, as role model, as literary artist, as author of a puzzling and persevering classic-- all continue. With each interpretation we see a different facet of Louisa May Alcott and, perhaps more importantly, a variant profile of ourselves.

In this reference guide I have made an exhaustive attempt to include all scholarship of any substance on Louisa May Alcott. I have not included foreign criticisms, unless translated into English.

Introduction

Despite repeated attempts, some newspaper citations have been unavailable for examination and have been included with references to source citations. Unless biographies contributed a new path or angle of critical approach, they have not been discussed in depth. Many reviews have been included in order to provide a sense of the contemporary public response and agreement or disagreement with the values and societal modes revealed in the books. I have not restricted myself to complete objectivity but have inserted subjective interpretations where I felt they would aid in clarifying the changing critical patterns.

Items have been listed chronologically, omitting years for which there were no critical treatments. The index has been planned to provide the utmost assistance to scholars who hope to use the volume for retrieval of desired information. I have included the names of members of the Alcott family, of authors of significant critical treatments, and of authors and titles of important biographical and bibliographical works. All Alcott titles treated in critical books and articles have been included with all pertinent items listed. I have also listed the major thematic patterns and topics revealed in the criticism. It is my hope that future scholars may find useful the guides provided to areas of potential examination.

In the months devoted to the compilation of this book I have incurred many debts of gratitude for assistance. I wish to thank Bowling Green State University for the research grant which permitted me to search out obscure sources. Dorothy Schmidt has provided invaluable assistance in research; she has been, in truth, a collaborator. Joan Conrad has been indispensable in her assistance in preparing the manuscript and in her encouragement in moments of stress. I owe particular gratitude to three staff members of the Bowling Green State University Library: Angela Poulos, Head of Collection Development, and Kausalya Raj and Catherine Sandy of the Interlibrary Loan Department, who were so efficient and willing in their efforts to obtain material. I owe personal thanks to the staffs of the Houghton Library, Harvard University, the Boston Public Library, the Boston Athenaeum, and the Concord Free Library. Ms. Virginia Haviland and other staff members of the Library of Congress gave me enthusiastic interest and willing assistance. For previously unlisted entries I wish to thank Dr. James Harner, a colleague, Ms. Anne Tracy of Michigan State University Library, and Freda Baum and Martha Shull, graduate students who also wrote about Louisa May Alcott. H. Glendon Steele has been helpful in assuring correct form. Finally, I wish to thank Dr. Jack Salzman, my editor and friend, for his patience and understanding.

Writings by Louisa May Alcott

BOOKS

Flower Fables. Boston: George W. Briggs, 1855.

Hospital Sketches. Boston: James Redpath, 1863.

The Rose Family. A Fairy Tale. Boston: James Redpath, 1864.

Moods. Boston: Loring, 1865; Revised edition. Boston: Roberts, 1882.

The Mysterious Key, and What It Opened. Boston: Elliott, Thomes and Talbot, 1867. Reprinted in Stern, Behind a Mask, 1975.

Morning-Glories, and Other Stories. Boston: Horace B. Fuller, 1868.

Kitty's Class Day. Boston: Loring, 1868.

Aunt Kipp. Boston: Loring, 1868.

Psyche's Art. Boston: Loring, 1868.

Three Proverb Stories. Boston: Loring, 1868.

Little Women or, Meg, Jo, Beth and Amy. Boston: Roberts, 1868.

Little Women or, Meg, Jo, Beth and Amy. Part Second. Boston: Roberts, 1869.

Hospital Sketches and Camp and Fireside Stories. Boston: Roberts, 1869.

An Old-Fashioned Girl. Boston: Roberts, 1870

Little Men: Life at Plumfield with Jo's Boys. London: Sampson Low, 1871.

Writings by Louisa May Alcott

My Boys. Aunt Jo's Scrap-Bag, 1. Boston: Roberts, 1872.

Shawl-Straps. Aunt Jo's Scrap-Bag, 2. Boston: Roberts, 1872.

Work: A Story of Experience. Boston: Roberts, 1873.

Something To Do. London: Ward, Lock, 1873.

Cupid and Chow-Chow. Aunt Jo's Scrap-Bag, 3. Boston: Roberts,
    1874.

Eight Cousins; or, The Aunt-Hill. Boston: Roberts, 1875.

Beginning Again. Being a Continuation of "Work." London: Sampson
    Low, 1875.

Silver Pitchers: And Independence, A Centennial Love Story.
    Boston: Roberts, 1876.

Rose in Bloom. A Sequel to "Eight Cousins." Boston: Roberts, 1876.

A Modern Mephistopheles. No Name Series. Boston: Roberts, 1877.
    Reprinted in A Modern Mephistopheles and A Whisper in the Dark.
    Boston: Roberts, 1889.

Under the Lilacs. Boston: Roberts, 1878.

My Girls. Aunt Jo's Scrap-Book, 4. Boston: Roberts, 1878.

Water Cresses. New York: Crowell, 1879.

Jimmy's Cruise in the Pinafore. Aunt Jo's Scrap-Bag, 5. Boston:
    Roberts, 1879.

Meadow Blossoms. New York: Crowell, 1879.

Jack and Jill. A Village Story. Boston: Roberts, 1880.

The Christmas Tree. London: George Routledge and Sons, 1881.

Proverb Stories. Boston: Roberts, 1882.

An Old-Fashioned Thanksgiving. Aunt Jo's Scrap-Bag, 6. Boston:
    Roberts, 1882.

Spinning-Wheel Stories. Boston: Roberts, 1884.

Lulu's Library, 1. Boston: Roberts, 1886.

Jo's Boys and How They Turned Out. A Sequel to "Little Men."
    Boston: Roberts, 1886.

Writings by Louisa May Alcott

Lulu's Library, 2. Boston: Roberts, 1887.

A Garland for Girls. Boston: Roberts, 1888.

Lulu's Library, 3. Boston: Roberts, 1889.

Recollections of My Childhood's Days. London: Sampson Low, 1890.

Comic Tragedies Written by "Jo" and "Meg" and Acted by the "Little
    Women." Boston: Roberts, 1893.
        According to Madeleine Stern, written c. 1848.

Behind a Mask. Introduction by Madeleine Stern. New York: William
    Morrow, 1975.
        Contains "Behind a Mask or a Woman's Power," "Pauline's Pas-
    sion and Punishment," "The Mysterious Key and What It Opened,"
    and "The Abbot's Ghost, or Maurice Treherne's Temptation."

SHORT FICTION

"The Rival Painters. A Tale of Rome." Olive Branch, 17, no. 19
    (8 May 1852).
        Published anonymously.

"The Rival Prima Donnas." Saturday Evening Gazette, Series for 1854,
    no. 45 (11 November 1854).
        Published under the pseudonym Flora Fairfield.

"The Little Seed," in Margaret Lyon, or A Work for All. Boston:
    Crosby, Nichols, 1854.

"A New Year's Blessing." Saturday Evening Gazette, Quarto Series,
    no. 1 (5 January 1856).

"The Sisters' Trial." Saturday Evening Gazette, Quarto Series, no. 4
    (26 January 1856).

"Little Genevieve." Saturday Evening Gazette, Quarto Series, no. 13
    (29 March, 1856).

"Bertha." Saturday Evening Gazette, Quarto Series, nos. 16-17
    (19-26 April 1856).

"Mabel's May Day." Saturday Evening Gazette, Quarto Series, no. 21
    (24 May 1856).

"The Lady and the Woman." Saturday Evening Gazette, Quarto Series,
    no. 40 (4 October 1856).

Writings by Louisa May Alcott

"Ruth's Secret." Saturday Evening Gazette, Quarto Series, no. 49 (6 December 1856).

"Mark Field's Mistake." Saturday Evening Gazette, 45, no. 11 (12 March 1859).

"Mark Field's Success." (Sequel to "Mark Field's Mistake.") Saturday Evening Gazette, 45, no. 16 (16 April 1859).

"Love and Self-Love." The Atlantic Monthly, 5, no. 29 (March 1860).

"A Modern Cinderella: or, The Little Old Shoe." The Atlantic Monthly, 6, no. 36 (October 1860).

"The King of Clubs and the Queen of Hearts." The Monitor, 1, nos. 1-7 (19 April-7 June 1862).

"Pauline's Passion and Punishment." Frank Leslie's Illustrated Newspaper, 15, nos. 379-380 (3-10 January 1863). Reprinted in Stern, Behind a Mask, 1975.

"M. L." The Commonwealth, 1, nos. 21-25 (24 January-22 February 1863).

"Hospital Sketches." The Commonwealth, 1, nos. 38-39, 41, and 43 (22-29 May and 12, 26 June 1863).

"Debby's Debut." The Atlantic Monthly, 12, no. 70 (August 1863).

"My Contraband; or, The Brothers." The Atlantic Monthly, 12, no. 73 (November 1863).

"A Hospital Christmas." The Commonwealth, 2, nos. 19-20 (8-15 January 1864).

"The Hospital Lamp." The Daily Morning Drum Beat, nos. 3-4 (24-25 February 1864).

"A Golden Wedding: and What Came of It." The Commonwealth, 2, nos. 35-36 (29 April-6 May 1864).

"Enigmas." Frank Leslie's Illustrated Newspaper, 18, nos. 450-451 (14-21 May 1864).
    Anonymous.

"Love and Loyalty." The United States Service Magazine, 2, nos. 1-3, 5-6 (July-September, November-December 1864).

"An Hour." The Commonwealth, 3, nos. 13-14 (26 November-3 December 1864).

"V. V.: or, Plots and Counterparts." <u>The Flag of Our Union</u>, 20, nos. 5-8 (4-25 February 1865). Reprinted as ten-cent novelette by A. M. Barnard. Boston: Thomes and Talbot, 1865. Anonymous.

"Nelly's Hospital." <u>Our Young Folks</u>, 1, no. 4 (April 1865).

"A Marble Woman: or, The Mysterious Model." <u>The Flag of Our Union</u>, 20, nos. 20-23 (20 May-10 June 1865). By A. M. Barnard.

"Behind a Mask: or, A Woman's Power." <u>The Flag of Our Union</u>, 21, nos. 41-44 (13 October-3 November 1866). Reprinted in Stern, <u>Behind a Mask</u>, 1975.

"The Abbot's Ghost: or, Maurice Traherne's Temptation." <u>The Flag of Our Union</u>, 22, nos. 1-4 (5-26 January 1867). Reprinted in Stern, <u>Behind a Mask</u>, 1975.

"What the Bells Saw and Said." <u>Saturday Evening Gazette</u>, 53, no. 51 (21 December 1867).

"The Skeleton in the Closet," in Perley Parker, <u>The Foundling</u>. Boston: Elliott, Thomes and Talbot, 1867.

"Tilly's Christmas." <u>Merry's Museum</u> [new series] 1, no. 1 (January 1868).

"My Little Friend." <u>Merry's Museum</u>, 1, no. 2 (February 1868).

"Our Little Newsboy." <u>Merry's Museum</u>, 1, no. 4 (April 1868).

"Will's Wonder-Book." <u>Merry's Museum</u>, 1, nos. 4-11 (April-November 1868).

"The Baron's Gloves." <u>Frank Leslie's Chimney Corner</u>, 7, nos. 160-163 (20 June-11 July 1868).

"The Blue and the Gray, A Hospital Sketch." <u>Putnam's Magazine</u>, 1, no. 6 (June 1868).

"A Royal Governess." <u>The Independent</u>, 20, no. 1023 (9 July 1868).

"My Polish Boy." <u>The Youth's Companion</u>, 41, nos. 48-49 (26 November-3 December 1868).

"Tessa's Surprise." <u>Merry's Museum</u>, 1, no. 12 (December 1868).

"Sunshiny Sam." <u>Merry's Museum</u>, 1, no. 12 (December 1868).

Writings by Louisa May Alcott

"Lost in a Pyramid; or, The Mummy's Curse." The New World, 1, no. 1 (16 January 1869).

"Back Windows." Merry's Museum, 2, no. 1 (January 1869).

"Dan's Dinner." Merry's Museum, 2, no. 2 (February 1869).

"A Curious Call." Merry's Museum, 2, no. 2 (February 1869).

"Perilous Play." Frank Leslie's Chimney Corner, 8, no. 194 (13 February 1869).

"A Visit to the School-Ship." Merry's Museum, 2, no. 3 (March 1869).

"The Little Boats." Merry's Museum, 2, no. 4 (April 1869).

"What Fanny Heard." The Youth's Companion, 42, no. 19 (13 May 1869).

"Milly's Messenger." Merry's Museum, 2, no. 5 (May 1869).

"A Little Gentleman." Merry's Museum, 2, no. 6 (June 1869).

"My Fourth of July." Merry's Museum, 2, no. 7 (July 1869).

"Madame Cluck and Her Family." Merry's Museum, 2, no. 8 (August 1869).

"A Marine Merry-making." Merry's Museum, 2, no. 10 (October 1869).

"Little Things." The Youth's Companion, 43, no. 3 (20 January 1870).

"Becky's Christmas Dream." Merry's Museum, 3, no. 1 (January 1870).

"Uncle Smiley's Boys." The Youth's Companion, 43, nos. 5-6 (3-10 February 1870).

"Mother's Trial." The Youth's Companion, 43, no. 21 (26 May 1870).

"Kate's Choice." Hearth and Home, 4, nos. 2-3 (13-20 January 1872).

"Shawl Straps." The Christian Union, 5, nos. 12-15 (13 March-3 April 1872).

"Cupid and Chow-Chow." Hearth and Home, 4, nos. 20-21 (18-25 May 1872).

"Pelagie's Wedding." The Independent, 24, no. 1227 (6 June 1872).

"The Romance of a Summer Day." The Independent, 24, no. 1239 (29 August 1872).

"Grandma's Team." The Youth's Companion, 45, no. 48
    (28 November 1872).

"Work; or Christie's Experiment." The Christian Union, 6, nos 26-27;
    7, nos. 1-25 (18-25 December 1872; 1 January-18 June 1873).

"The Mystery of Morlaix." The Youth's Companion, 45, no. 51
    (19 December 1872).

"Bonfires." The Youth's Companion, 46, no. 2 (9 January 1873).

"Huckleberry." The Youth's Companion, 46, no. 3 (16 January 1873).

"Mamma's Plot." The Youth's Companion, 46, no. 6 (6 February 1873).

"Little Boston." The Youth's Companion, 46, no. 24 (12 June 1873).

"Seven Black Cats." The Youth's Companion, 46, no. 31 (31 July 1873).

"Anna's Whim." The Independent, 25, no. 1291 (28 August 1873).

"Transcendental Wild Oats." The Independent, 25, no. 1307
    (18 December 1873).

"Patty's Place." Young Folks' Journal, 3, nos. 11-12
    (January-February 1874).

"A Happy Birthday." The Youth's Companion, 47, no. 6
    (5 February 1874).

"Roses and Forget-Me-Nots." St. Nicholas, 1, no. 5 (March 1874).

"Lost in a London Fog." The Youth's Companion, 47, no. 15
    (9 April 1874).

"Little Neighbors." Hearth and Home, 6, nos. 15-16
    (11-18 April 1874).

"Dolly's Bedstead." The Youth's Companion, 47, no. 18
    (30 April 1874).

"What the Girls Did." The Youth's Companion, 47, no. 20
    (14 May 1874).

"How I Went Out to Service. A Story." The Independent, 26,
    no. 1331 (4 June 1874).

"A Little Cinderella." The Youth's Companion, 47, no. 26
    (25 June 1874).

Writings by Louisa May Alcott

"London Bridges." The Youth's Companion, 47, no. 30 (23 July 1874).

"The Autobiography of an Omnibus." St. Nicholas, 1, no. 12 (October 1874).

"Tribulations Travels." The Youth's Companion, 48, no. 3 (21 January 1875).

"Red Tulips." The Youth's Companion, 48, no. 8 (25 February 1875).

"What a Shovel Did." The Youth's Companion, 48, no. 15 (15 April 1875).

"Silver Pitchers, A Temperance Tale." The Youth's Companion, 48, nos. 18-23 (6 May-10 June 1875).

"By the River." The Independent, 27, no. 1384 (10 June 1875).

"Old Major." The Youth's Companion, 48, no. 31 (5 August 1875).

"My Little School-Girl." The Youth's Companion, 48, no. 44 (4 November 1875).

"Letty's Tramp." The Independent, 27, no. 1412 (23 December 1875).

"Marjorie's Birthday Gifts." St. Nicholas, 3, no. 3 (January 1876).

"A New Way To Spend Christmas." The Youth's Companion, 49, no. 10 (9 March 1876).

"Helping Along." St. Nicholas, 3, no. 5 (March 1876).

"Only an Actress." Demorest's Monthly Magazine, 12, no. 4 (April 1876).

"A Visit to the Tombs." The Youth's Companion, 49, no. 21 (25 May 1876).

"Clams, A Ghost Story." The Youth's Companion, 50, no. 18 (3 May 1877).

"Clara's Idea." The Youth's Companion, 50, no. 37 (13 September 1877).

"Mrs. Gay's Prescription." The Woman's Journal, 9, no. 34 (24 August 1878).

"John Marlow's Victory." The Independent, 30, no. 1568 (19 December 1878).

"Two Little Travellers." St. Nicholas, 6, no. 8 (June 1879).

"How It All Happened." Harper's Young People, 2, no. 60
    (21 December 1880).

"An Old-Fashioned Thanksgiving." St. Nicholas, 9, no. 1
    (November 1881).

"My Red Cap." The Sword and Pen, 1, nos. 1-4 (7-10 December 1881).

"A Country Christmas." The Independent, 33, nos. 1724-1725
    (15-22 December 1881).

"Number Eleven." The Youth's Companion, 55, no. 33 (17 August 1882).

"A Christmas Dream." Harper's Young People, 4, nos. 162-163
    (5-12 December 1882).

"Grandmamma's Pearls." St. Nicholas, 10, no. 2 (December 1882).

"Little Pyramus and Thisbe." St. Nicholas, 10, nos. 11-12
    (September-October 1883).

"Sophie's Secret." St. Nicholas, 11, nos. 1-2 (November-
    December 1883).

"Bertie's Box. A Christmas Story." Harper's Young People, 5,
    no. 218 (1 January 1884).

"Grandma's Story." St. Nicholas, 11, no. 3 (January 1884).

"Tabby's Table-Cloth." St. Nicholas, 11, no. 4 (February 1884).

"Eli's Education." St. Nicholas, 11, no. 5 (March 1884).

"Onawandah." St. Nicholas, 11, no. 6 (April 1884).

"Little Things." St. Nicholas, 11, no. 7 (May 1884).

"The Banner of Beaumanoir." St. Nicholas, 11, no. 8 (June 1884).

"Jerseys, or The Girl's Ghost." St. Nicholas, 11, no. 9
    (July 1884).

"The Little House in the Garden." St. Nicholas, 11, no. 10
    (August 1884).

"Daisy's Jewel-Box and How She Filled It." St. Nicholas, 11, no. 11
    (September 1884).

"Corny's Catamount." St. Nicholas, 11, no. 12 (October 1884).

"The Cooking-Class." St. Nicholas, 12, no. 1 (November 1884).

Writings by Louisa May Alcott

"The Hare and the Tortoise." St. Nicholas, 12, nos. 2-3
  (December 1884-January 1885).

"Baa! Baa!" Harper's Young People, 6, nos. 307-308
  (15-22 September 1885).

"The Candy Country." St. Nicholas, 13, no. 1 (November 1885).

"A Christmas Turkey, and How It Came." Harper's Young People, 7,
  no. 321 (22 December 1885).

"The Blind Lark." St. Nicholas, 14, no. 1 (November 1886).

"Little Robin." Harper's Young People, 8, no. 371 (7 December 1886).

"What It Cost." The Young Crusader, 1, no. 6 (11 February 1887).

"A Flower Fable." The Woman's Journal, 18, no. 9 (26 February 1887).

"An Ivy Spray." St. Nicholas, 14, no. 12 (October 1887).

"The Silver Party." Harper's Young People, 9, no. 421
  (22 November 1887).

"Pansies." St. Nicholas, 15, no. 1 (November 1887).

"The Little Red Purse." Harper's Young People, 9, no. 423
  (6 December 1887).

"Trudel's Siege." St. Nicholas, 15, no. 6 (April 1888).

"Lu Sing." St. Nicholas, 30, no. 2 (December 1902).

"The Eaglet in the Dove's Nest." St. Nicholas, 30, no. 3
  (January 1903).

"A Christmas Dream and How It Came True." Colliers, 126
  (23 December 1950).

SHORT NON-FICTION (SELECTED)

"With a Rose, That Bloomed on the Day of John Brown's Martyrdom."
  (A poem.) The Liberator, 30, no. 3 (20 January 1860).

"Thoreau's Flute." (A poem.) The Atlantic Monthly, 12, no. 71
  (September 1863).

"Happy Women." The New York Ledger, 24, no. 7 (11 April 1868).

Writings by Louisa May Alcott

"Mr. Emerson's Third Lecture." National Anti-Slavery Standard, 29,
no. 26 (31 October 1868).

"Women in Britanny." The Christian Register, 51, no. 1
(6 January 1872).

"Hope for Housekeepers." Boston Transcript, 46, no. 14
(13 November 1873).

"Letter of Miss Louisa Alcott." The Woman's Journal, 5, no. 46
(14 November 1874).

"Woman's Part in the Concord Celebration." The Woman's Journal, 6,
no. 18 (1 May 1875).

"Letter from Louisa M. Alcott." The Woman's Journal, 7, no. 29
(15 July 1876).

"Letter to N.W.C.T.U." Our Union, 3, no. 6 (November 1877).

"Letter from Louisa M. Alcott." The Woman's Journal, 10, no. 41
(11 October 1879).

"Letter from Louisa M. Alcott." The Woman's Journal, 11, no. 14
(3 April 1880).

"Victoria. A Woman's Statue." Demorest's Monthly Magazine, 17,
nos. 3-5 (March-May 1881).

"Letter from Louisa M. Alcott." The Woman's Journal, 13, no. 6
(11 February 1882).

"Reminiscences of Ralph Waldo Emerson." The Youth's Companion, 55,
no. 21 (25 May 1882).

"W.C.T.U. of Concord." Concord Freeman, 10, no. 26 (30 June 1882).

"R. W. Emerson." Demorest's Monthly Magazine, 18, no. 9 (July 1882).

"Preface," in Prayers by Theodore Parker. Boston: Roberts, 1882.

"Mr. Alcott's True Condition." The Woman's Journal, 14, no. 1
(6 January 1883).

"Letter from Miss Alcott." The Woman's Journal, 14, no. 10
(10 March 1883).

"Letter from Miss Louisa M. Alcott." The Woman's Journal, 15,
no. 20 (17 May 1884).

Writings by Louisa May Alcott

"In Memoriam Sophia Foord." The Woman's Journal, 16, no. 15
    (11 April 1885).

"Miss Alcott on Mind-Cure." The Woman's Journal, 16, no. 16
    (18 April 1885).

"Old Times at Old Concord." The Woman's Journal, 16, no. 16
    (18 April 1885).

"When Shall Our Young Women Marry?" The Brooklyn Magazine, 4, no. 1
    (April 1886).

"Early Marriages." Ladies' Home Journal, 4, no. 10 (September 1887).

"A Sermon without a Text," in What Can a Woman Do? By Mrs. M. L.
    Rayne. Detroit: Dickerson, 1887, pp. 435-437.

"Recollections of My Childhood." The Youth's Companion, 61, no. 21
    (24 May 1888).

Writings about Louisa May Alcott

1854

1. ANON. Review of Flower Fables. Boston Evening Transcript
   (19 December).
   Describes Flower Fables as "agreeable sketches" and feels
   the book is suited to "the capacity of intelligent young
   persons."

2. ANON. Review of Flower Fables. Saturday Evening Gazette
   (20 December).
   Misnames book "Flower Tables" but finds the fairy stories
   "very sweet."

1863

1. ANON. Review of Hospital Sketches. Boston Transcript. (See
   Alcott Papers, Houghton Library).
   Favorable treatment; calls the volume "fluent and sparkling"
   with "touches of quiet humor"; speaks of the "uncommon merit"
   of the work.

*2. ANON. Review of Hospital Sketches. Liberator.
   Praises the book as a work of excellence. Cited in Stern,
   Louisa May Alcott, 1950.3.

*3. ANON. Review of Hospital Sketches. Waterbury American.
   Favorable review describes the incidents as "graphically
   drawn." Cited in Stern, Louisa May Alcott, 1950.3.

1865

1. ANON. Review of Moods. Harper's Weekly (21 January).
   Calls it "a short story of great power and absorbing interest" by a new writer whose "Hospital Sketches" were "remark-
   able for a humor and insight which ought to have made them

1865

more widely known." Comments on the "conflict of passion in
noble characters" as being "drawn with great delicacy and
skill, and with a freedom and firmness which promise remark-
able works hereafter." Concludes by saying, "After Hawthorne
we recall no American love-story of equal power."

2. ANON. Review of Moods. Reader (April).
    Calls it "transcendental literature." Recorded in Journals
    (April 1865), 166.

3. JAMES, HENRY. Review of Moods. North American Review, 101
    (September), 276-281. Reprinted in Notes and Reviews
    [Cambridge, Mass.: Dunster House, 1921] 57-58.
    Calls plot silly with "too much coincidence," but praises
    her imagination and terms last half of book "replete with
    beauty and vigor." Claims the "authoress has derived her
    figures . . . from the depths of her moral consciousness,"
    although limited "experience of human nature" hampers reality,
    characters possess "certain beauty and grace."

1868

*1. ANON. Review of Little Women 1. American Literary Gazette,
    12, no. 1 (2 November), 16.
    Cited in Stern, Louisa May Alcott, 1950.3.

*2. ANON. Review of Little Women, 1. Arthur's Illustrated Home
    Magazine (December), 375.
    Cited in Stern, Louisa May Alcott, 1950.3.

*3. ANON. Review of Little Women, 1. Godey's Lady's Book, 77,
    no. 462 (December), 546.
    Cited in Stern, Louisa May Alcott, 1950.3.

*4. ANON. Review of Little Women, 1. The Ladies Repository, 28
    (December), 472.
    Cited in Stern, Louisa May Alcott, 1950.3.

*5. ANON. Review of Little Women, 1. The Lady's Friend, 5, no. 12
    (December), 857.
    Cited in Stern, Louisa May Alcott, 1950.3.

6. ANON. Review of Little Women, 1. Nation, 7 (22 October), 335.
    Sees the book as "not only very well adapted to the readers
    for whom it is especially intended but [as one which] may also
    be read with pleasure by older people."

*7. ANON. Review of <u>Little Women, 1</u>. <u>The Youth's Companion</u>, 41, no. 43 (22 October).
   Cited in Stern, <u>Louisa May Alcott</u>, 1950.3.

1869

*1. ANON. Review of <u>Little Women, 2</u>. <u>The Commonwealth</u>, 7, no. 34 (24 April).
   Cited in Stern, <u>Louisa May Alcott</u>, 1950.3.

2. ANON. Review of <u>Little Women, 2</u>. <u>Harper's</u>, 39 (August), 455–456.
   Regards the book as "a rather mature book for the little women, but a capital one for their elders."

3. ANON. Review of <u>Little Women, 2</u>. <u>Nation</u>, 8 (20 May), 400.
   Recognizes Alcott's success as parallel to that of her character Jo in being based on family life, but warns that this success may "endanger its author's pretensions to do better work in the future."

*4. ANON. Review of <u>Little Women, 2</u>. <u>National Anti-Slavery Standard</u>, 29, no. 52 (1 May).
   Cited in Stern, <u>Louisa May Alcott</u>, 1950.3.

1870

1. ANON. Review of <u>An Old-Fashioned Girl</u>. <u>Athenaeum</u>, 2225 (18 June), 803.
   Calls work bright, spirited, and wholesome but hopes young people exaggerated so that like fashions will never prevail in England.

2. ANON. Review of <u>An Old-Fashioned Girl</u>. <u>The Atlantic Monthly</u>, 250 (June), 752–753.
   Criticizes work for bad grammar and poor writing.

3. ANON. Review of <u>An Old-Fashioned Girl</u>. <u>Godey's Lady's Book</u>, 80 (June), 576.
   Acclaims work a "book of the month," but cites resemblance to <u>Little Women</u>.

4. ANON. Review of <u>An Old-Fashioned Girl</u>. <u>Godey's Lady's Book</u>, 81 (September), 281.
   Prefers work to its predecessors as <u>Old-Fashioned Girl</u> "talks less slang."

1870

5. ANON. Review of An Old-Fashioned Girl. Godey's Lady's Book, 81
       (November), 472.
          Suggests that "dash of vulgarity" and hardness in lives of
       city cousins may reflect Alcott's "unfortunate" experience of
       Boston life, but finds books popular because of reality of
       characters.

6. ANON. Review of An Old-Fashioned Girl. Harper's, 41 (June), 144.
          Considers book more popular than Little Women with an older
       audience, but wonders whether it represents an "uprising
       against the tyrannical reign of Mrs. Grundy."

7. ANON. Review of An Old-Fashioned Girl. Lippincott's, 6
       (August), 230-231.
          Praises work as "uncommon enough to warrant particular
       eulogy" because of its "delicate and faithful portraiture"
       and "simple, graceful and modest style," as well as a "decided
       acknowledgment of . . . mental and moral worth." Calls writing
       honest and fearless.

8. ANON. Review of An Old-Fashioned Girl. Nation, 11 (14 July),
       30-31.
          Finds no really good writers for and about children in
       America. Alcott is "as good as any" but is guilty of being
       "Bostonian" in her portrayal of young children. Many of her
       portrayals are "strictly true to nature" but are too often
       used to point a moral. An Old-Fashioned Girl is pleasing
       but cannot be predicted to be "pleasing of more generations
       than one."

9. ANON. Review of An Old-Fashioned Girl. New Orleans Times
       Picayune (17 April), p. 12.
          Claims story has interest enough to carry to close, but is
       informed by "woman's rights motif . . . by no means so pro-
       nounced as to dominate the harmony of its composition."

1871

1. ANON. Review of Little Men. Athenaeum, 2278 (24 June), 781.
          Calls novel a description of the impossible, having same
       relationship to school systems as More's Utopia had to
       politics.

2. ANON. Review of Little Men. Godey's Lady's Book, 83 (August),
       186.
          Sees Alcott as "decidedly the children's author as Miss
       Edgeworth was years ago."

3. ANON. Review of <u>Little Men</u>. <u>Harper's</u>, 43 (August), 458.
   Calls book entertaining but lacking in plot and movement.
   Criticizes the type of education presented, an educational
   philosophy based on that of her father, but admits that book
   encourages that sympathetic relationship with children which
   is the "first condition" of their care and nurture.

4. ANON. Review of <u>Little Men</u>. <u>Overland Monthly and Out West
   Magazine</u>, 7 (September), 293.
   Finds <u>Little Men</u> as enjoyable as <u>Little Women</u> and filled
   with insightful, natural characterizations, a true sympathy
   for children and "truthful illustrations of the power of their
   imagination."

<u>1872</u>

1. ANON. Review of <u>Aunt Jo's Scrap Bag</u>. <u>Athenaeum</u>, 2341
   (7 September), 303.
   Reviews this "collection of fugitive tales and sketches
   with some shock at parent/child role reversal in 'Tessa's
   Surprise.'"

2. ANON. Review of <u>Aunt Jo's Scrap Bag</u>. <u>Harper's</u>, 44 (February),
   463.
   Describes book as "mirth-provoking" for children, and
   possibly subject to disapproval by "serious-minded parents,"
   especially the chapter "The Children's Joke."

<u>1873</u>

1. ANON. Review of <u>Aunt Jo's Scrap Bag</u>. <u>Godey's Lady's Book</u>, 86
   (February), 187.
   Describes Alcott's writings as natural, witty, full of
   invention and character.

2. ANON. Review of <u>Shawl Straps</u>. <u>Harper's</u>, 46 (March), 616.
   Affirms Alcott's well-known style as "always vivacious,
   but not always natural and simple." Calls this a travel book
   under the guise of fiction.

3. ANON. Review of <u>Work</u>. <u>Athenaeum</u>, 2342 (26 July), 111.
   Calls story restless, fatiguing and depressing. Feels that
   "a little bit of happiness would have been much better for
   everybody."

1873

4. ANON. Review of <u>Work</u>. <u>Godey's Lady's Book</u>, 87 (September), 284.
    Views it as an experiment by Miss Alcott in writing a long
    story upon her favorite subject. Traces the plot, finding its
    moral in the quotation on the title page: "An endless signif-
    icance lies in work, in idleness alone is there perpetual
    despair."

5. ANON. Review of <u>Work</u>. <u>Harper's</u>, 47 (September), 618-619.
    Criticizes book as being "without even the semblance of a
    plot" in the first half; sees it as not a novel at all, but
    "a serious didactic essay on the subject of woman's work."
    Despite external defects, sees "sunny cheerfulness infused
    through all its pages." Concludes, "The book would not have
    made her reputation, but her reputation will make the book."

1874

1. ANON. Review of <u>Aunt Jo's Scrap Bag</u>. <u>Godey's Lady's Book</u>, 87
    (February), 186.
    Speaks of Alcott's style as being in that "peculiar vein
    which interests alike children and those of older growth."
    Finds a wealth of incident, good character presentation, and
    appealing verisimilitude. Particularly praises "Nelly's Hos-
    pital" and "Cupid and Chow-Chow."

1875

1. ANON. Review of <u>Eight Cousins</u>. <u>Athenaeum</u>, 2504 (23 October),
    538-539.
    Considers Alcott's sympathies as belonging to children
    rather than adults. Sees her working within "the little
    allotment she has appropriated in the morning-land of child-
    hood" where her stories are "healthy" presentations of such
    problems as "woman's real mission" so well illustrated in
    <u>Eight Cousins</u>.

2. ANON. Review of <u>Eight Cousins; or The Aunt-Hill</u>. <u>Godey's Lady's
    Book</u>, 91 (December), 570.
    Praises Alcott's style as pleasant and easy, with "an even
    flow of interest." Finds the boy characters "a little too
    good for real life" and their dialogue not always "the real
    thing." However, "there is so much that is good and bright
    in the story" that such things are trifles. Wishes that all
    children's books were as healthy in tone.

3. ANON. Review of <u>Eight Cousins</u>. <u>Overland Monthly and Out West Magazine</u>, 15 (November), 493-494.
    Finds typical Alcott "vigor, discrimination, character-portraiture, and racy dialogue." Eagerly awaits the sequel which will appeal to "children of a larger growth."

4. JAMES, HENRY. "Eight Cousins: or the Aunt-Hill." <u>Nation</u>, 21 (14 October), 250-251. Reprinted, <u>see</u> 1957.6.
    Finds Alcott's book "unfortunate not only in its details but in its general tone, in the constant ring of its style." Registers alarm at Alcott's sympathy with the earthy attitudes, taste and language of those children who made a habit of putting adults in their place. Attacks lack of "charm" of American children, finding in this book no glow, no fairies, but only "rather vulgar prose."

1876

1. ANON. Review of <u>Rose in Bloom</u>. <u>Literary World</u>, 7 (December), 104.
    Sees book as weakened by "the worm of sickly sentiment . . . growing at its heart" and made unreal by "torturing" the hearts of children with the "agonies of love." Commends book, however, as one of her best and improved in style.

2. ANON. Review of <u>Rose in Bloom</u>. <u>Nation</u>, 23 (21 December), 373.
    States that <u>Rose</u> is sequel to <u>Eight Cousins</u>, and carries readers through courtship to the "utmost verge of fiction for minors."

3. ANON. Review of <u>Silver Pitchers</u>. <u>Athenaeum</u>, 2346 (12 August).
    Acknowledges "pretty temperance tale" with American young ladies under "condition of American society . . . . somewhat different from our own."

4. ANON. Review of <u>Silver Pitchers</u>. <u>Harper's</u>, 53 (September), 629.
    Mentions "Silver Pitchers" as a "capital temperance tale, quite different from the ordinary pattern of melodramatic misery."

5. ANON. Review of <u>Silver Pitchers</u>. <u>Nation</u>, 23 (25 July), 45.
    Calls collection "of lightest weight" but finds "Transcendental Wild Oats" entertaining.

1877

1. ANON. Review of <u>A Modern Mephistopheles</u>. <u>The Atlantic Monthly</u>, 40 (July), 109.
    Guesses that author is Julian Hawthorne; calls book "a remarkable one and instinct with ability" in which there is a "signal force of some kind."

2. ANON. Review of <u>A Modern Mephistopheles</u>. <u>Godey's Lady's Book</u>, 95 (July), 86.
    Guesses that author is a girl with "literary facility and fluency" but little knowledge of life. When older and more experienced "the author may make her mark."

3. A. W. H. Review of <u>A Modern Mephistopheles</u>. <u>Library Table</u>, 3 (27 September), 185.
    Comments on contrast between cold tone at beginning changing gradually to glowing eloquence at end. Calls it a study rather than a novel.

4. BURLINGAME, EDWARD R. Review of <u>A Modern Mephistopheles</u>. <u>North American Review</u>, 125 (September), 316-318.
    Claims "unknown author" writes with both "defects and merits of a woman's pen." Calls book allegorical and imaginative, a "fresh and dainty fantasy" albeit somewhat too romanticized.

5. ANON. Review of <u>Rose in Bloom</u>. <u>New Orleans Times-Picayune</u> (4 February), p. 6.
    Likes the book because it is written "sensibly, simply and with a pretty vivacity." Presents a "strong natural picture of young life."

1878

1. ANON. Review of <u>Under the Lilacs</u>. <u>New Orleans Daily Picayune</u> (8 December), p. 5.
    Regards Alcott as supreme in writing for children.

2. ANON. Review of <u>Under the Lilacs</u>. <u>Rose Belford's Canadian Monthly Review</u> (November), p. 637.
    Praises Alcott's naturalness and "sprightliness and vigour" of style. Approves of absence of "goody-goody padding" but notes the "genuine impression for good."

3. ANON. Review of <u>Under the Lilacs</u>. <u>Saturday Review</u>, 46 (30 November), 700.

Finds characters "childlike and healthy-minded" but to English readers the social relationships are "somewhat strange."

1879

1. ANON. Review of Aunt Jo's Scrap Bag. Nation, 29
    (18 December), 427.
    Condemns fifth volume as "unreal and sentimental writing" and unwholesome family reading.

2. ANON. Review of Under the Lilacs. New Orleans Times-Picayune
    (16 February), p. 11.
    Finds author and characters "charming." Sees appeal to children and adults alike.

1880

1. PARTON, JAMES. Eminent Women: A Series of Sketches of Women Who Have Won Distinction by Their Genius and Achievements as Authors, Artists, Actors, Rulers, or within the Precincts of Home. New York: International Book, pp. 78-90. Reprinted, see 1885.2.
    Records Alcott's description of her first sales to the Saturday Evening Gazette, her hospital experiences, and the publication of volume 1 of Little Women in Paris with an ending invented by the French translator.

1881

1. ANON. Review of Jack and Jill. The Atlantic Monthly, 47
    (January), 123-124.
    Objects to "unfailing success of every character," lack of character development, and "the suppressed love-making" of the young characters. Expresses dilemma of reviewers with question, "we object to the blood-and-thunder literature, and when in place of it we have the milk-and-sugar we object again. What do we want?"

1882

1. ANON. Review of Proverb Stories. Saturday Review, 54
    (9 December), 774.

1883

> Sees stories as not suited to English children because of too much "love-making." Stories classed as didactic although they are told in "a bright, picturesque way."

1883

1. HANAFORD, PHEBE A. Daughters of America. Augusta, Me.: True, pp. 227-228.
    Recounts Alcott's refusal to make speech at Vassar, and same action at Sorosis Club.

1884

1. ANON. Review of Spinning Wheel Stories. Nation, 39 (4 December), 487.
    Contains brief acknowledgment of "variety, spirit and good feeling" expected in Alcott stories.

1885

1. MOULTON, LOUISE CHANDLER. "Louisa Mae Alcott," in Our Famous Women. Hartford: Worthington, pp. 29-52.
    Discusses Alcott's work habits and autobiographical content of her books. Identifies Theodore Parker as "Mr. Power" of Work, and Alcott as "Christie." Quotes Alcott as believing in transmigration.

2. PARTON, JAMES. Daughters of Genius. Philadelphia: Hubbard, pp. 78-90. Reprint of 1880.1.

1886

1. ANON. Review of Jo's Boys. New York Times (26 October), p. 10:2.
    Hails the return of Miss Alcott and rejoices in renewing acquaintance with "the bright boys and girls who peopled her pages." Recounts the "not wholly imaginary" ordeals of Mrs. Bhaer as a famous writer whose life and home are invaded by admirers of all ages. Details the final position in life of the characters who appear for "the last, the very, very last" time.

2. ANON. Review of Lulu's Library. Saturday Review, 62 (3 July), 727.

Briefly describes this latest work written "of little children for little children." English children might have difficulty with idiomatic expressions but generally universality is evident.

3. BOLTON, SARAH K. <u>Lives of Girls Who Became Famous</u>. New York: Crowell. Reprinted, <u>see</u> 1949.1.
   Recounts Alcott's life as independent, fun-loving prototype of her character Jo March. Written for juveniles, article presents glowing appreciation of Bronson's skills as an educator and reports Louisa's exuberant joy on occasion of her first publication. Subsequent edition, <u>see</u> 1925.1.

1888

1. ANON. Review of <u>A Garland for Girls</u>. <u>The Critic</u>, 12, (11 February), 67.
   Praises this publication, the last collection to be reviewed during Alcott's life.

2. CHENEY, EDNAH D. <u>Louisa May Alcott: The Children's Friend</u>. Boston: L. Prang.
   First Cheney tribute stresses Alcott's interest in and influence upon children readers. Lacks the important primary material found in the second work, <u>Life, Letters and Journals</u>, 1889.2.

3. HARLOW, LURABEL. <u>Louisa May Alcott: A Souvenir</u>. Boston: Sam E. Cassino.
   Highly sentimental account of Louisa's relationship to her father and other members of the family. Wonders at the lack of transcendentalism in Louisa's work which revealed the struggle between "ideality" and necessity. Reveals contemporary appreciation of <u>Hospital Sketches</u> and of <u>Little Women</u>, with <u>Old-Fashioned Girl</u> and <u>Little Men</u> next in order. Gives minute details of death and burial of Louisa May Alcott.

1889

1. ANON. "Miss Alcott's Stern Life Battle." <u>New York Times</u> (14 October), p. 3:1.
   Reviews Cheney's <u>Louisa May Alcott: Her Life, Letters and Journals</u>. Lauds book for revelation of bravery and cheerfulness of Alcott's life and her total dedication to family. Quotes extensively from book.

1889

2. CHENEY, EDNAH D. <u>Louisa May Alcott: Her Life, Letters, and
    Journals</u>. Boston: Roberts. Reprinted, <u>see</u> 1928.1.
         Shaped critical interpretation until 1940s with selections
    emphasizing autobiographical nature of Alcott's "best" work.
    Portrays Alcott as "Duty's Child." Preserves Alcott poems as
    chapter headings. Records events and attitudes as only a
    family friend could do. Important in shaping the "Alcott
    myth."

3. HOLLOWAY, LAURA CARTER (LANGFORD). <u>The Woman's Story</u>. New York:
    Alden, pp. 482-501.
         Contains two-page biography and portrait, with reprint of
    "Transcendental Wild Oats," selected by Alcott just before her
    death.

1890

1. ANON. Review of <u>Louisa May Alcott: Her Life, Letters and
    Journals</u>. <u>The Atlantic Monthly</u>, 65 (March), 420.
         Describes Cheney's biography as an "unstudied, almost
    fragmentary memoir." Alcott's life seems representative of
    New England girlhood, but she is seen as "ruthlessly beating
    against the cage, yet showing almost a fierce solicitude for
    all its similarly imprisoned companions." Sees great possi-
    bilities lost in Alcott's career.

2. ANON. Review of <u>Louisa May Alcott: Her Life, Letters and
    Journals</u>. <u>The Critic</u>, 17 (25 October), 202.
         Sees Ednah Cheney's biography as revealing a woman greater
    than all of her works because "she wrote for bread, and with a
    rapidity too great for the best work." Concludes that the
    biography reveals "rare discrimination and sound judgement,
    and . . . true appreciation of her subject."

1891

1. ANON. "Miss Alcott's Birthplace." <u>The Critic</u>, 18 (10 January),
    22.
         Brief letter to editor of Germantown <u>Telegraph</u> describes
    "Pine Place" in Germantown, Pa. where Louisa May Alcott was
    born. Also recounts Amos Bronson Alcott's educational experi-
    ments which led to his failure and removal to Boston where
    "his advanced thought" found greater sympathy.

2. LAZARUS, JOSEPHINE. "Louisa May Alcott." <u>Century</u>, 42 (May),
    59-67.

Quotes copiously from Cheney. Calls Alcott undisturbed by
"any sentimental proclivities or longings," with her heart "a
clear crystal well, reflecting the calm family affections, the
free, active, and yet contained existence that is equal to its
own needs and the needs of others." Suggests that greater
powers of imagination might have carried her works into
"higher flight."

1892

1. PORTER, MARIA S. "Recollections of Louisa May Alcott." New
    England Magazine, 6 (March), 2-19.
    Provides valuable personal accounts of conversations with
    Louisa May Alcott, dealing with her pride in her ancestry,
    the influence of her father and friends, and of such events
    as the Fruitlands experiment. Presents Louisa May Alcott as
    a "ruthless" critic of her society, an advocate of woman suf-
    frage and college education for women, and the possessor of a
    keen and caustic sense of humor. Recounts final illnesses and
    deaths of father and daughter.

1893

1. ANON. Review of Comic Tragedies. New York Times (5 November),
    p. 19:4.
    Sees little value in the collection of melodramas written
    and performed by the Alcott girls. Cannot understand the
    attitude of Meg, the editor, that "it was perfectly natural
    for children living in a Massachusetts hamlet . . . to write
    plays in fun that have all the bloodthirsty spirit and roman-
    tic symbolism of the old school of melodrama and to act the
    parts in them in those leisure hours when children might be
    better employed playing games of romp in the open air." Sees
    the volume as, at best, a curiosity.

2. PORTER, MARIA S. Recollections of Louisa May Alcott, John
    Greenleaf Whittier, and Robert Browning, Together with Several
    Memorial Poems. Boston: New England Magazine. Includes
    reprint of 1892.1.

3. SANBORN, FRANK B. and W. T. HARRIS. Amos Bronson Alcott: His
    Life and Philosophy. Boston: Roberts. Reprinted 1965 by
    New York: Biblo and Tannen Booksellers and Publishers.
    Vol. 2, pp. 458-524 passim.
    Important because of relationship between Amos Bronson and
    Louisa May Alcott. Indicates father's encouragement from 1854

1895

when he published her earliest Flower Fables. Sanborn published Louisa's letters from Washington as "Hospital Sketches"
in Boston Commonwealth (22 May-26 June 1863) and records that
they "ran like wildfire through the country, and were copied
in many newspapers." Quotes Louisa's surprise at this success and her later description of Little Women as succeeding
because "we really lived most of this book."

1895

1. STEARNS, FRANK P. Sketches from Concord and Appledore. Concord
   Thirty Years Ago. New York: Putnam, pp. 66-88.
   Describes Bronson Alcott as "one of nature's gentlemen" who
   lived a blameless if somewhat ineffectual life. Characterizes
   Louisa Alcott as a May, practical and strong-minded. Finds
   her "simple pictures of domestic country life are drawn with
   a firm and confident hand," but Alcott herself had a "broad
   cosmopolitan mind" which was constrained in Concord environs.

1896

1. THAYER, WILLIAM M. Women Who Win or Making Things Happen.
   New York: Nelson.
   Contains chapter on "Louisa May Alcott--Story-teller."
   Generally favorable, praising Alcott's ability to achieve
   despite barriers.

1898

1. ANON. "Books That Separate Children from Their Parents." New
   York Times Saturday Review of Books and Art (8 January), p. 18.
   Decries the established pattern of "children's books"
   which tend further to widen the gulf between children and
   parents. "The world of books should be common ground."
   Quotes a statement by a mother: "I am sorry to be obliged
   to be sorry that Miss Alcott ever wrote." Insists that the
   truly influential books are the great classics intended for
   all.

2. FURMAN, DOROTHY. Review of Ednah Cheney's Louisa May Alcott:
   Her Life, Letters and Journals. New York Times Saturday Review of Books and Art (9 April), p. 238.
   Quotes extensively from the book, terming it more valuable
   for its ethical lessons than for its literary style.

1901

3. M. L. S. "A Word for Miss Alcott." New York Times/Saturday
    Supplement (26 February), p. 14:2.
        In answer to 1898.1, this mother's letter defends Alcott's
    works. Insists that Little Women and others united parents
    and children who read them. Sees them as having "a pure,
    healthy tone, and embodying examples of unselfishness, cheer-
    fulness and hopefulness in spite of disappointments and mis-
    fortunes." Finds them much more realistic than stories of
    "that little prig" Elsie Dinsmore.

1899

1. WHITING, LILIAN. "Louise [sic] May Alcott." Chautauquan, 29
    (June), 280.
        Recollections of a visit to Amos Bronson Alcott's School of
    Philosophy in 1881 and first meeting with Louisa May Alcott.
    Found her full of "courage and magnetism" and a "unique per-
    sonality." Presents her life as one of "duty" and her books
    as "transcriptions" rather than "creations." Alcott used her
    literature to "invigorate and to elevate life." Traces her
    life and the influences which made its impact much larger than
    that of a traditional literary figure.

1900

1. GOULD, ELIZABETH LINCOLN. "Little Men, Dramatized." Ladies'
    Home Journal, 18 (December), 3-4.
        This two-act, forty-five-minute play was adapted from
    Alcott's work by Elizabeth Lincoln Gould. It is generously
    illustrated by Reginald B. Birch, illustrator of "Little Lord
    Fauntleroy." Obviously intended for amateur production by
    children, it succeeds in capturing the tone and personalities
    of the original.

1901

1. BARRETT, WENDELL. A Literary History of America. London:
    T. Fisher Unwin.
        States that Little Women "does for the '60's what Rollo
    does for the '40's": gives a picture of "New England
    Characteristics."

2. EARLE, MARY TRACY. "A New Edition of Little Men." Book Buyer,
    23 (December), 380.
        Thirty years have proved lasting popularity. All Alcott
    stories "turn on such simple human motives that they cannot

1901

soon be out of date." This new edition is attractive but
illustrations are too "fairylandish" for Alcott's "real" boys
and girls.

3. GOULD, ELIZABETH LINCOLN. The "Little Women" Play a Two-Act Play
   Adapted from Louisa May Alcott's Story. Ladies' Home Journal,
   18 (January), 3-4, 37-38.
       Intended for amateur production, selected events in the
   lives of the "Little Women" before the death of Beth. Illustrations by Reginald B. Birch.

4. WHITMAN, ALFRED. "Letters to Her Laurie." Ladies' Home Journal,
   18 (16 September), 5-6 and (11 October), 6.
       Includes parts of twelve letters from Louisa May Alcott to
   Whitman. Reveals that Laurie in Little Women was a combina-
   tion of Whitman and Louisa's Polish boy, Ladislas. Concludes
   that Louisa, "caught in the web of fame," tried "to find her
   own soul, while easing the life of her beloved family." Once
   again sounded notes of duty and rebellion.

1902

1. BACON, E. M. "Alcotts and Their Homes." Literary Pilgrimages.
   New York: Silver Burdett, pp. 387-402.
       Recounts early family history of Alcotts and describes life
   at Hosmer Cottage, Fruitlands, the Hillside, and Orchard House.
   Adulatory account of Louisa's work, although erroneous date of
   her death.

2. CLARK, ANNIE M. L. The Alcotts in Harvard. Lancaster, Mass.:
   J. C. L. Clark.
       Another set of personal reminiscences.

3. "Lu Sing." St. Nicholas, 30 (December), 128-135.
       Prints story from "Lulu's Library" with introduction by
   Annie Alcott Pratt concerning origin of tale.

1903

1. "Portrait." Education, 23 (April), 496.
       Reproduction of a bust of Louisa May Alcott and a single
   mention of Elwell's sculpture.

2. PRATT, ANNIE ALCOTT. "About Little Women." St. Nicholas, 30
   (May), 631. Reprinted, see 1932.14.
       Presents possibly edited letter.

1905

1. ANON. Review of Jack and Jill and Under the Lilacs. Outlook, 81 (21 October), 428.
   Describes Jack and Jill as a "portrayal of home and school life in a New England village, full of Miss Alcott's unconventional good spirits." Gives merely a brief narrative account of Under the Lilacs.

2. ANON. Review of Under the Lilacs. Nation, 81 (16 November), 406.
   Claims that slang and "untidy English" of earlier books have become less offensive; but claims "amateur lovemaking" is a "distinct blot" better "postponed" for boys and girls, although Under the Lilacs is termed better than most in this respect.

3. ANON. Review of Under the Lilacs. Review of Reviews, 32 (December), 32.
   Praises the standard of writing in this reprint, saying that it is "supreme because it is natural." The "fantastical, dramatic, or sentimental point" is set against a background of simplicity.

4. BEACH, SETH CURTIS. Daughters of the Puritans. Boston: American Unitarian Association. Reprinted, see 1967.1.
   Calls Alcott the "most popular story-teller for children, in her generation." Highly derivative of the Journals. Calls Work "one of the most deservedly popular of her books." One of the first to comment on Alcott's suffrage activity.

1906

1. GREEN-ARMYTAGE, A. J. Maids of Honor: Twelve Descriptive Sketches of Single Women Who Have Distinguished Themselves in Philanthropy, Nursing, Poetry, Travel, Science, Prose. Edinburgh and London: Blackwood.
   One chapter on Louisa May Alcott, laudatory but contributes nothing new.

2. SANBORN, FRANK B. "Women of Concord." The Critic, 48 (April), 338–350.
   Considers the impact of Concord upon Louisa May Alcott and her relationship to the New England setting.

3. SMITH, S. D., JR. "Jack and Jill; Dialogue." Ladies' Home Journal, 24 (December), 14, 73.
   Contains "A Louisa Alcott Play for Christmas."

1907

<u>1907</u>

1. ASHMUN, M. "On a Portrait of Miss Alcott." (A poem.) <u>New England Magazine</u>, 37 (September), 78.
   Child's concept of Alcott as one untouched by time gives way to humanity revealed by portrait.

2. CHESTERTON, G. K. "Louisa Alcott." <u>Nation</u>. Reprinted, <u>see</u> 1953.1. (Not seen.)

<u>1908</u>

1. SANBORN, FRANK B. <u>Bronson Alcott at Alcott House, England, and Fruitlands, New England: 1842-1844</u>. Cedar Rapids, Iowa: Torch Press.
   Contains brief discussion by Louisa May Alcott.

<u>1909</u>

1. ANON. Review of <u>Little Women</u>. <u>Bookman</u> (London) 37 (Christmas Supplement December), 80.
   Hails the illustrations by M. V. Wheelhouse for a new edition of the classic, which differentiate characters and retain the "home-charm" which made <u>Little Women</u> famous.

2. GOWING, CLARA. <u>The Alcotts As I Knew Them</u>. Boston: C. M. Clark.
   Contains personal reminiscences of the entire Alcott family. Similar to many others with little new.

3. MOSES, BELLE. <u>Louisa May Alcott, Dreamer and Worker: A Story of Achievement</u>. New York: D. Appleton.
   Makes use of passages from Cheney's <u>Life, Letters and Journals</u> but also includes selected comments by Alcott's contemporaries such as Dr. Edward Emerson and Nathaniel Hawthorne. Examines the majority of Alcott's writings and includes known details of publication; thus, departs from purely reminiscent tone of earlier treatments.

<u>1910</u>

1. ANON. Review of <u>The Louisa Alcott Story Book</u>. <u>New York Times</u>, (8 October), p. 553.
   Sees "happy little tales" as useful supplementary reader for young children.

2. HOLLAND, RUPERT. Historic Girlhoods. Philadelphia: Jacobs,
   pp. 291-302.
       Calls Alcott "The Girl of Concord" and records children's
   impromptu dramas in fictionalized account.

1911

1. ANON. "To Preserve the Home of the Author of Little Women as a
   Memorial." New York Times (25 June), V, p. 15:1.
       Calls Concord centre of pilgrimage for American literature
   and its great men, but lauds Alcott as "strongest, stoutest,
   bravest man among them all," for her life was writing.

2. GEROULD, KATHARINE F. "Miss Alcott's New England." The Atlantic
   Monthly, 108 (August), 180-186. For expanded reprint see
   1920.1.
       Emphasizes Alcott's work as a cultural mirror of her con-
   temporary New England.

1912

1. LOGAN, MRS. JOHN A. (MARY S.), ed. The Part Taken by Women in
   American History. Wilmington, Del.: The Perry-Nalle Publishing Co., pp. 798-799.
       Brief biographical sketch; does include the pseudonymous
   works in periodicals, Hospital Sketches and support of woman
   suffrage. States that "no one has done more for the women of
   her own generation than she."

2. SANBORN, FRANK B. "Reminiscences of Louisa May Alcott."
   Independent, 72 (7 March), 496-502.
       The author, one of the original Concord transcendentalists,
   sees the dramatization of Little Women as delayed recognition
   of the dramatic predilections of Louisa May Alcott. Traces
   Louisa's dramatic experiences through biographical recollections of the entire family.

1913

1. ABBOT, WILLIS J. Notable Women In History. Philadelphia:
   Winston, pp. 362-366.
       Commends Alcott's suffragist views, but attributes her
   claim to history to her writing. Calls her "militant" and the
   "architect of her own fortunes" despite poverty and illness.

1914

1. BONSTELLE, JESSIE and MARION DEFOREST. Little Women Letters
   from the House of Alcott. Boston: Little, Brown.
      Contains some writing by Louisa May Alcott, material
   valuable for later biographies.

2. STEEDMAN, AMY. When They Were Children. New York: F. A. Stokes,
   pp. 356-365.
      Offers saccharine accounts of some childhood incidents.

1915

1. HAWTHORNE, HILDEGARDE. "An Adventure with Little Women."
   Delineator, 86 (June), 8-10.
      Fanciful account of the return of two small girls to the
   world of Jo, heroine of Little Women. Excellent photographs
   add a touch of reality to fancy.

2. LINN, EDITH WILLIS and HENRY BAZIN. Alcott Memoirs Posthumously
   Compiled from Papers, Journals, and Memoranda of the Late
   Dr. Frederick L. H. Willis. Boston: Badger.
      Indicates a heightened awareness of the necessity to pre-
   serve Alcott primary sources.

3. PATTEE, FRED. History of American Literature since 1870.
   New York: Century.
      Points out the low state of American fiction in 1860s.
   Little Women listed as one of only thirteen American novels
   published during the seven years before 1870. Dismisses
   Alcott as one of a group of women novelists, more specifically,
   "daughters of the Brahmins."

4. SEARS, CLARA ENDICOTT, comp. Bronson Alcott's Fruitlands.
   Boston and New York: Houghton Mifflin; Cambridge: Riverside.
      Contains accounts by several Fruitlands visitors; excerpts
   from Louisa May Alcott's diary of that period with a few later
   annotations, and reprints "Transcendental Wild Oats."

5. WHITING, LILIAN. Women Who Have Ennobled Life. Philadelphia:
   Union Press.
      Chapter about Louisa May Alcott and her contributions and
   inspirational works.

1916

1. PICKETT, LASALLE (CORBELL). "Louisa May Alcott," in <u>Across My Path, Memories of People I Have Known</u>. New York: Brentano's. Reprinted, <u>see</u> 1970.7.

1917

1. CUNLIFFE, J. W. and A. H. THORNDIKE, eds. <u>Warner Library</u>. Vol. 1. New York: U.S. Publishing Associations, pp. 283-295.
    Contains selections from <u>Hospital Sketches</u>, <u>Little Women</u>, with brief critical essay.

2. DORLAND, W. A. NEWMAN. <u>The Sum of Feminine Achievement: A Critical and Analytical Study of Women's Contribution to the Intellectual Progress of the World</u>. Boston: The Stratford Company, pp. 189, 219.
    Classes Alcott as a juvenile story writer in "The Century of the Women" and claims "a remarkable vogue" for the <u>Little Women</u> series.

1918

1. SEYMOUR, G. S. "Home of Louisa May Alcott." <u>Photo-Era</u>, 40 (June), 308.
    A sentimental poem accompanying the photograph of Orchard House. Praises Alcott's lasting effect on child readers.

1919

1. ANON. "Books for Children." <u>Literary Digest</u>, 63 (29 November), 81.
    Quotes Amy Lowell as having been forbidden to read Alcott because of the work being "untrue to life" and using "very bad English." On later reading, Lowell endorsed those criticisms finding books not "valuable in any way."

2. ANON. "Little Women in London." <u>Literary Digest</u>, 63 (20 December), 31.
    Treats the stage version of <u>Little Women</u> in London very favorably. Finds Katharine Cornell's dramatization of "Jo" particularly fine. Points up the interesting war-provoked change of the nationality of Jo's husband from German to French.

1919

3. BRADFORD, GAMALIEL. "Portrait of Louisa May Alcott." <u>North</u>
    <u>American Review</u>, 209 (March), 391-403.
        Includes Alcott among Abigail Adams, Harriet Beecher Stowe,
    Frances Willard, and Emily Dickinson. Stresses her morality,
    apologizes for her literary worth, yet concludes by yoking her
    with Shakespeare in "giving profit and delight to millions."

4. BRADFORD, GAMALIEL. <u>Portraits of American Women</u>. New York:
    Houghton Mifflin, pp. 167-194.
        Very similar to treatment in <u>Portraits and Personalities</u>
    (1934.4), with identical ending. Does stress Alcott's moral-
    ity: "She rarely misses an opportunity for direct preaching."
    Describes her morality as humanitarianism rather than piety.

                            1920

1. GEROULD, KATHARINE F. "Miss Alcott's New England," in <u>Modes and</u>
    <u>Morals</u>. New York: Scribner's, pp. 182-198. Expands article
    with identical title, <u>see</u> 1911.2.
        Strongly anti-Victorian in tone. Sees Alcott as providing
    more documentary value than W. D. Howells; <u>Little Women</u> is an
    excellent contemporary record of manners and morals. True
    religion is lacking while morality is overwhelming. Reveals
    new interest in sociology as she analyzes relationships in
    Miss Alcott's families and between her characters and their
    fictional communities.

2. IVES, CHARLES EDWARD. <u>Essays before a Sonata</u>. New York:
    Knickerbocker Press, pp. 44-48.
        Contains four stanzas of musical composition entitled "The
    Alcotts." Quotes Concord character that best thing Bronson
    ever did was his daughters, despite fact that Louisa did not
    accept father as prototype, instead she left a "memory-word-
    picture of healthy New England childhood days."

                            1922

1. BRAZIL, ANGELA. "<u>Little Women</u>: An Appreciation." <u>The Bookman</u>
    (December), pp. 139-140.
        Explores the continuing popularity of <u>Little Women</u>.
    Praises realistic viewpoint, sense of humor, moral influence
    without "priggishness."

2. HAWTHORNE, JULIAN. "Woman Who Wrote Little Women." <u>Ladies' Home</u>
    <u>Journal</u>, 39 (October), 25, 120-124.
        Presents anecdotes from life in Concord by son of Alcotts'
    neighbor Nathaniel Hawthorne.

                            34

1923

*1. MOORE, REBECCA DEMING. When They Were Girls. Owen, 1923, 1937,
    pp. 22-29.
        Listed in Ireland, Index to Women, 1970.3.

2. NORTHEND, MARY H. "Some Memories of the Author of Little Women."
    St. Nicholas, 51 (November), 74-78.
        Briefly eulogizes Alcott; contains five photographs from
    Orchard House.

1924

*1. MACVEAGH, LINCOLN, ed. The New Champlin Encyclopaedia for Young
    Folks. New York: Holt, pp. 12-13.
        Listed in Ireland, Index to Women, 1970.3.

2. VINCENT, ELIZABETH. "Subversive Miss Alcott." New Republic, 40
    (22 October), 204.
        Asks why Alcott books are still classics in the midst of
    sensational fiction and films. Answers that little girls like
    moralizing; they have "a natural depraved taste" and "Miss
    Alcott panders to these passions."

1925

1. BOLTON, SARAH K. Lives of Girls Who Became Famous. New York:
    Crowell.
        New edition of 1886.3, enlarged from original. Contains
    chapter on "Louisa May Alcott."

2. CATHER, KATHERINE DUNLAP. Younger Days of Famous Writers. New
    York and London: Century, pp. 117-141.
        Intended for juvenile audience. Fanciful account of the
    beginning of Alcott's career.

1926

1. ADELMAN, JOSEPH. Famous Women. New York: Lonow, pp. 216-217,
    portrait.
        Calls her writing "typical in her social ethics" of father's
    literary generation. Quotes Lazarus on Louisa May Alcott's
    life of "unswerving purpose and will" overshadowing her works,
    see 1891.2.

Writings about Louisa May Alcott

2. BEER, THOMAS. The Mauve Decade. Garden City, New York: Garden
    City Publishing Co., pp. 17-27.
        Calls Alcott influential for generations of girls and
    women, but criticizes Bronson's improvidence. Indicative of
    decade's general attitude toward Amos Bronson Alcott.

3. BROWN, MARY HOSMER. Memories of Concord. Boston: Four Seas.
        Another reminiscent account of Louisa May Alcott's con-
    temporary Concord by a member of a family well known by
    Concord transcendentalists.

4. MORSE, KATHERINE. "Introduction," in Little Women or Meg, Jo,
    Beth and Amy. New York: Macmillan.
        Introduces brief biography with personal reminiscences of
    reading Little Women. Says Alcott "glorified spinsterhood."

5. ROWLAND, ARTHUR P. "Introduction," in Little Women.
    Philadelphia: Winston, pp. ix-xiii.
        Calls picture of New England life "intimate and accurate"
    and moral precepts as sound as ever to successive generations.

6. TICKNOR, CAROLINE, comp. Classic Concord. Boston: Houghton
    Mifflin.
        Contains examples of Louisa May Alcott's works relating to
    Concord.

1927

1. ANON. "Little Women Leads Poll." New York Times (22 March),
    p. 7:1.
        Rates Little Women ahead of the Bible for influence on
    high school pupils.

2. MORROW, HONORÉ WILLSIE. The Father of Little Women. Boston:
    Little, Brown.
        Examines father-daughter relationship but contains little
    that is new to readers of the journals by both father and
    daughter.

3. RAYMOND, CHARLES H. Story-Lives of Master Writers. New York:
    Stokes.
        Contains section, "Louisa May Alcott"; offers little that
    is new.

1928

1. CHENEY, EDNAH D. Louisa May Alcott: Her Life, Letters and
     Journals. Boston: Little, Brown. Reprint of 1889.2.
        Illustrated.

2. ROLLER, BERT. "When Jo Died." Sewanee Review, 36 (April–June),
     164–170.
        Describes briefly the last days of Alcott and criticizes
     funeral eulogy as being inappropriate for one "so intensely
     human, so spirited and brave."

1929

1. JOHNSON, M., comp. "American First Editions." Publishers Weekly,
     116 (19 October), 1965–1966.
        Lists first editions of Alcott books. Valuable for col-
     lectors and for textual study.

2. MAHONY, BERTHA E. and ELINOR WHITNEY. Realms of Gold in Chil-
     dren's Books. New York: Doubleday, pp. 601–603.
        Quotes both Louisa May Alcott and Ednah Cheney to show
     Alcott's devotion to family.

3. MANN, DOROTHEA LAWRANCE. "When the Alcott Books Were New."
     Publishers Weekly, 116 (28 September), 1619–1624.
        Describes the continued status of Alcott books as best-
     sellers, especially Little Women. Gives a brief, rather
     superficial account of the life and career of Louisa May
     Alcott. Gives a detailed account of the Roberts Brothers'
     edition of 1868 and recounts the many translations in Europe
     as well as in Greece and China in later years. Notes that the
     American Library Convention in June 1922 voted Little Women
     first on a list of twenty-five books considered best for a
     one-room country school.

4. MARTIN, HELEN, ed. Aunt Jo's Scrap Bag. Boston: Little, Brown.
        Election of seventeen stories from the original seven vol-
     umes with explanatory introduction.

5. TICKNOR, CAROLINE. May Alcott/A Memoir. Boston: Little, Brown.
        Much personal reminiscence but does reveal details of
     Louisa's popularity in Europe as illustrated by contacts dur-
     ing European tour. "Louisa's fame reaches over the seas and
     makes a welcome for us everywhere." Adds dimension to the
     prototype of one of the "Little Women."

1929

6. TURNER, LORENZO DOW. "Louisa May Alcott's 'M. L.'" Journal of
    Negro History, 14 (October), 495-522.
        Contains reprint of "M. L." from Boston Commonwealth,
    January-February 1863. One of the first twentieth-century
    recognitions of Louisa May Alcott's abolitionism.

                                1930

1. LESLIE, EVA G. Lulu's Library. Boston: Little, Brown.
        Presents nine stories "selected mainly . . . because they
    contain delicate flights of fancy and promising bits of color
    description."

2. PARRINGTON, VERNON. The Beginnings of Critical Realism. New
    York: Harcourt-Brace.
        Erroneous index reference to "the grotesque vaporings of
    Alcott" really refers to Amos Bronson Alcott.

3. STARBUCK, EDWIN D., et. al. A Guide to Books for Character.
    Vol. 2. New York: Macmillan.
        Recommends Alcott's book for teaching character. Classifies
    works by attitudes and situations which provide moral instruc-
    tion for children.

                                1931

1. KEYES, ROWENA K. Lives of Today and Yesterday/A Book of Compara-
    tive Biography. New York: D. Appleton, pp. 219-233. Reprint
    of section of 1909.3.
        Details Louisa's life in Concord from age thirteen until
    the publication of Little Women.

2. SKINNER, RICHARD DANA. "Little Women: Criticism." Commonweal,
    15 (23 December), 215.
        Brief review of William A. Brady's revival of Little Women.
    Describes the play as "a respite from the dreary plays of the
    hour" which brings back "something of simplicity, charm and
    dignified beauty."

3. WINTERICH, JOHN T. "Romantic Stories of Books, Little Women."
    Publishers Weekly, 120 (15 August), 607-611.
        Contains standard biographical information with brief com-
    ments on value of first editions of Little Women.

1932

1. AHLERS, LENA C. <u>Daughters Known to Fame</u>. Chicago: Whitman, pp. 15-20.
   Contains brief biography for juveniles.

2. ANON. "Alcott Centenary." <u>Publishers Weekly</u>, 122 (27 August), 677.
   Suggests appropriate activities for celebration of Alcott centennial in bookstores, schools, and libraries.

3. ANON. "<u>Little Women</u> Relive in Old Alcott Home." <u>New York Times</u> (30 November), p. 22:2.
   Recounts the centenary celebration of Louisa May Alcott held at Old Orchard House in Concord. Among the guides were two women who were intimates of the Alcott household. Also present was Mrs. Frederick Alcott Pratt, wife of the nephew of Louisa May Alcott.

4. ANON. "Louisa M. Alcott Centenary Year." <u>Publishers Weekly</u>, 122 (2 July), 23-25.
   Lists sales of Alcott books by centennial year of her birth; includes brief genealogy of fictional March family.

5. ANON. "When Louisa M. Alcott Wrote for the Journal." <u>Ladies' Home Journal</u>, 49 (November), 96.
   Contains quotations from earlier writings of Alcott for <u>Ladies' Home Journal</u>, first published there in September 1887.

6. CLOUTER, F. M. <u>Saturday Review of Literature</u>, 9 (19 November), 260.
   Announces publication of Gulliver bibliography (<u>See</u> 1932.10) and describes the extensive and widespread celebration of the Alcott Centenary. Describes Ms. Gulliver's Boston Public Library collection of all editions of American, English, and foreign origin, along with "personalia."

7. EATON, ANNE T. "The Author of 'Little Women' and Children's Books Today." <u>New York Times Book Review</u> (13 November), p. 8+.
   As the title suggests, the books read by the Alcott girls are contrasted to the books read by modern children. Lists many books published in 1932, with frequent reference to Alcott and <u>Little Women</u>. Feels that two "new types" would appeal to Louisa May Alcott: books on science and picture books made possible by modern technology.

1932

8. GOLDSMITH, SOPHIE L. "Jo and Her Books." St. Nicholas, 60
   (November), 26–27.
   Claims Alcott is loved as her books are loved because she
   is her books.

9. GOLDSMITH, SOPHIE L. "Louisa Alcott and Children's Books."
   Nation, 135 (23 November), 510.
   Acclaims Alcott's "eager awareness," "courage and cheerfulness," "real story-telling sense," passionate love of children,
   and delight in home life. Lists recommended books for children representing these qualities.

10. GULLIVER, LUCILE. Louisa May Alcott/A Bibliography. With an
    appreciation by Cornelia Meigs. Boston: Little, Brown.
    In this important work all known editions are described
    with annotations useful for critical purposes. Ms. Meigs
    praises Alcott's "courageous candor" and her picture of "youth
    adapting itself to life as it unfolds."

11. HILLYER, LAURIE. "Marmee." Parent's Magazine, 7 (November),
    23–24, 42–43.
    Includes previously unpublished letter from Louisa to a
    friend containing her description of her mother's life and
    character.

12. "Julian Hawthorne's Memories of Old Concord Days When Louisa
    Alcott Did Not Take Her Talents Seriously." New York Times
    Book Review (27 November), p. 11.
    An interesting recollection of Louisa May Alcott by
    Nathaniel Hawthorne's son, who, although fourteen years
    younger, enjoyed with her a "boy-and-young woman friendship,
    happy and wholesome," a friendship which continued until
    Louisa's death. He recalls Amos Bronson Alcott who was a
    total failure but lucky in three things: being the husband
    of Miss May, the father of Louisa, "his best contribution to
    literature," and a friend of Emerson. He imagines the chil-
    dren in heaven reading Little Women and clustering around
    Louisa while, in the sun parlor, Plato, Emerson, and Alcott
    converse. Describes the charming young Louisa with a penchant
    for tricks yet a deep sympathy for all. The personal, touch-
    ing account closes with a requiem for a past which could never
    return and a present which would be unrecognizable to "another
    race" which peopled the Concord of his youth.

13. Portrait. Publishers Weekly, 122 (5 November), 1775.
    Mentions portraits supplied by publisher for centennial.

14. PRATT, ANNIE ALCOTT. "A Letter from Meg." St. Nicholas, 60
    (November), 27.
        Replies to letter (1871) of Alcott admirer, describing
    correspondence of Alcott sisters to March characters. Although
    headnote claims letter was "never before published," it is
    almost verbatim 1903.2.

15. ROBBINS, L. H. "Honor to Louisa Alcott." New York Times Book
    Review (11 October), pp. 16-18.
        Presents Alcott as "a greater heroine than any that she
    portrayed." In a lavishly illustrated article the early hard-
    ships of the family are chronicled. Special emphasis is placed
    on the Fruitlands experience and on Louisa's struggles preced-
    ing the publication of Little Women.

                                1933

1. ANON. Review of film Little Women. New York Times (26 November),
    IX, p. 4:2.
        Traces background of writing books; notes that Katharine
    Hepburn plays Jo.

2. ANON. Review of Invincible Louisa. Atlantic Bookshelf,
    Vol. 152 (September), p. 10.
        Biography reveals a growing, changing personality, not a
    static representative of another age. This Alcott was far in
    advance of her time and knew "the differences between 'moral
    pap' and the living word."

3. BECKER, MAY LAMBERTON. Review of Invincible Louisa. Books
    (4 June), p. 7.
        Praises the inclusion of new material and the creativity
    with which many resources were melded into an original whole.

4. BRADFORD, GAMALIEL. Portraits and Personalities. Edited by
    Mabel A. Bessey. Boston: Houghton Mifflin. Reprinted, see
    1968.2.
        Short biographies intended for high school students. Sees
    Alcott ridden by an "ideal." Doesn't see her as artistic in
    tastes but regards her mode of composition, her moods, her
    depressions as "of the artist." Stresses her extensive use
    of personal experience. Compares her to Shakespeare in giving
    profit and delight to millions. See 1919.4.

5. EATON, A. T. Review of Invincible Louisa. New York Times
    (11 June), p. 11.

1933

Points out the "American quality" which the books of Alcott
and Cornelia Meigs share. Biography marked by integrity,
"fine reserve and dignity."

6. "Letter from Louisa M. Alcott to Viola Price Franklin."
   Overland Monthly [new series], 91 (August), 106.
   Letter to personal acquaintance describes Louisa M.
   Alcott's failing health. Dated Boston, 18 December 1885, the
   letter tells of her limited ability to write, her desire for
   solitude, her reading and writing habits. States that she
   takes "heroes and heroines from real life--much truer than
   any one can imagine." Details the many letters asking her
   for money and advice. Urges that Mrs. Franklin teach her
   students "to love books but to let authors rest in peace."

7. MEIGS, CORNELIA L. The Story of the Author of Little Women/
   Invincible Louisa. Boston: Little, Brown. Reprinted, see
   1968.16.
   One of the better Alcott biographies. Reveals Alcott in
   her relationship to her family and friends, the houses in
   which she lived, and her steadfast confrontation of a diffi-
   cult life. Not a critical evaluation of works, but provides
   background valuable for an understanding of the works.

8. REID, DOROTHY E. "Booklovers' Corner." St. Nicholas, 60
   (September), sup. 2+.
   Calls Little Women "brewed of truth and laughter and phi-
   losophy, stirred up by the ladle of genius."

9. SHEA, A. L. Review of Invincible Louisa. Chicago Daily Tribune
   (18 November), p. 14.
   Calls it "a classic which will take its place beside that
   of Little Women."

1934

1. ADLOW, DOROTHY. "Louisa Alcott's Sister May." Christian Science
   Monitor, 26 (29 August), 10.
   Discusses influence of French art and such artists as
   Turner upon Alcott's sister whose art was "personal and
   domestic." Feels that May's resolve "to be an attractive
   and accomplished woman even if she never became a great
   artist" would present an ideal for women "who take too seri-
   ously to brush and pigment."

2. CARNEGIE, DALE. Little Known Facts about Well-Known People.
   New York: The World's Work, pp. 185-187, portrait.

Records phenomenal response to motion picture <u>Little Women</u> as unequaled in New York. Gathers negative anecdotes concerning Louisa's attitude toward her writing.

3. HARTWICK, HARRY. <u>The Foreground of American Fiction</u>. New York: American Book Co.
     Describes "polite fiction" in 1890s as consisting "mainly of 'moral pap for the young,' as Louisa May Alcott described her own stories. . . ."

4. KUNITZ, STANLEY J. and HOWARD HAYCRAFT. <u>The Junior Book of Authors</u>. Introduction by Effie L. Power. 1st edition. New York: H. W. Wilson.
     An introduction to lives of writers and illustrators for younger readers, with photos and drawings.

1935

1. ANON. "Cobbler Recalls Emerson, Hawthorne." <u>New York Times</u> (22 December), p. 14:4.
     Recalls providing shoes for Alcotts and other literary greats.

2. ANON. "Famous Shoe Buyers." <u>New York Times</u> (24 December), p. 14:4.
     Refutes cobbler's claim of having shod Concord literary lights. Suggests faulty memory rather than deliberate fraud.

*3. FITZHUGH, HARRIET LLOYD and PERCY K. FITZHUGH. <u>Concise Biographical Dictionary</u>. New York: Grosset and Dunlap, pp. 12-13.
     Listed in Ireland, <u>Index to Women</u>, 1970.3.

1936

1. ANON. Review of <u>Louisa Alcott's People</u>. London <u>Times Literary Supplement</u> (21 November), p. 971.
     Favorable commentary.

2. ANON. Review of <u>Louisa Alcott's People</u>. <u>Springfield Republican</u> (29 November), p. 7e.
     Favorable review of content and illustrations by Thomas Fogarty.

3. ANTHONY, KATHARINE S. "The Happiest Years." <u>North American Review</u>, 241 (June), 297-310.

43

1936

Evidently an early version of sections of her later biography, in particular the thirteenth to sixteenth years of Louisa May Alcott's life. Some generalizations seem to have little or no factual basis. Calls Concord the "democracy of genius" in which the Alcotts spent their "golden age."

4. BECKER, MAY LAMBERTON. *Louisa Alcott's People*. New York: Scribner's.
   An original and creative arrangement of characters from Alcott books.

5. BENET, WILLIAM ROSE. Review of *Louisa Alcott's People*. *Saturday Review of Literature*, 15 (14 November), 22.
   Favorable review, commenting on selection of material and on illustrations by Thomas Fogarty.

6. MCDOWELL, MAUDE APPLETON. "Louisa May Alcott: Reminiscences by the Original Goldilocks." *St. Nicholas*, 64 (November), 29+.
   Acknowledges *Little Men* and *Little Women* films; offers random childhood reminiscences of Alcott.

1937

1. ANTHONY, KATHARINE S. "Most Beloved American Writer." *Woman's Home Companion*, 64 (December), 9-11+; 65 (January), 11-13; 65 (February), 9-11+; 65 (March), 20-22+.
   Serializes Anthony psychobiography of Louisa May Alcott, see 1938.3.

2. Portrait. *Saturday Review of Literature*, 15 (27 March), II, 12.
   Photograph shows Louisa Alcott at her desk.

1938

1. ADAMS, MILDRED. "When the Little Angels Revolted." *New York Times Magazine* (6 March), p. 10+.
   Effectively compares the worlds of children in 1868 and 1938, finding the "stuff of greatness" which causes Alcott's books to remain popular. Suggests that James's panning of the books was typical of attitude of that era that children wanted "only what was good for them."

2. ANTHONY, KATHARINE S. "Letter to the Editor." *Yale Review*, 27 (June), 861-862.
   Replies to negative reviews of her biography, claiming that she had been influenced in her interpretations by "original

pages of the diaries from which Cheney's <u>Life, Letters and Journals</u> were taken."

3. ANTHONY, KATHARINE S. <u>Louisa May Alcott</u>. New York: Knopf.
    In this psychoanalytic biography, Anthony examines "the psychic wounds" which affected the lives of the Alcott family. Resulted in a spate of controversial reviews. Serialized, <u>see</u> 1937.1.

4. BLANCK, JACOB N. "Alcott's 'An Old-Fashioned Girl'/A Collation." <u>Publishers Weekly</u>, 133 (19 February), 967.
    Deals with technical details of the first edition existing in three variants. Describes color, format, illustrations and advertisements.

5. CANBY, HENRY SEIDEL. "Louisa in the Laboratory." <u>Saturday Review of Literature</u>, 17 (12 February), 12.
    Reviews Anthony's biography negatively because of psychological interpretation. Claims misinterpretation of transcendentalists and of relationship between Mrs. Alcott and Charles Lane.

6. CRISMAN, GRACE. "Louisa's Father and Bronson's Daughter." <u>Scholastic</u>, 32 (5 March), 21-22.
    Rather superficial treatment of the mixed effect of Amos Bronson Alcott's reform teachings on Louisa May. Sees their ideas as inseparable. Calls "Transcendental Wild Oats" most important result of Fruitlands experiment.

7. FISHER, DOROTHY CANFIELD. "Understanding Aunt Louisa." <u>Survey Graphic</u>, 27 (May), 289.
    Positive review of Anthony biography. Stresses that real meaning of Alcott's life was duty.

8. GEISMAR, MAXWELL. "Duty's Faithful Child." <u>Nation</u>, 146 (19 February), 216.
    Typical in reviewing Katharine Anthony's <u>Louisa May Alcott</u>. Finds it readable but lacking in psychological insights and superficial in its exploration of the complicated relationships among the Alcotts. Sees Louisa as "the psychological whipping-boy for the social and domestic failures of her parents." Blames Victorian stress on duty. Claims "an excess of moral virtue is a psychological vice." Does see Anthony's as "the first mature biography of Louisa Alcott."

9. KUNITZ, STANLEY J. and HOWARD HAYCRAFT. <u>American Authors, 1600-1900: A Biographical Dictionary of American Literature</u>. New York: H. W. Wilson, pp. 18-19.
    Includes biography of Louisa May Alcott.

1938

10. SHEPARD, ODELL. The Journals of Bronson Alcott. Boston:
    Little, Brown.
       Presents a careful one-volume selection from the many hand-
    written volumes of Bronson Alcott's Journals. In part traces
    the growth of Louisa's literary career.

11. SHEPARD, ODELL. "Mother of Little Women." North American
    Review, 245 (June), 391-398.
       Reviews Katharine Anthony's Louisa May Alcott negatively.
    Sees Alcott as perennially adolescent, spurning abstract
    thought, popular because the American public is immature.
    Anthony's sexual "innuendos" concerning all of the Alcotts
    are irresponsible. Does praise Louisa's honesty and devotion
    and those other qualities for which "millions have loved her
    and love her still."

12. SHEPARD, ODELL. Pedlar's Progress: The Life of Bronson Alcott.
    Boston: Little, Brown.
       Contains laudatory biography of Bronson, yet credits Louisa
    with immortalizing the Alcott household through the March
    novels, despite her father's limited expectations for this
    dark, difficult child.

13. TALBOT, MARION. "Glimpses of the Real Louisa May Alcott." New
    England Quarterly (December), pp. 731-738.
       Denies Elizabeth Vincent's charge (see 1924.2) that Alcott
    did not like girls. Bases interpretation upon visits to and
    letters from Alcott. Claims Alcott's interest in education
    of girls, charitable work, welfare of working women and suf-
    frage. Denies Geismar's charge of Alcott's sterile life
    (see 1938.8). Suggests that the Cheney Life, Letters and
    Journals established a myth not fully supported by other
    evidence.

14. WINTERICH, JOHN T. Twenty-Three Books and the Stories behind
    Them. New York: J. B. Lippincott, pp. 195-204.
       After a brief biographical sketch, describes creation of
    manuscript and first edition. Details the problems of deter-
    mining the illustrator in the first edition of Little Women
    and of the original publication in two parts. Also describes
    the many English editions and variations.

1939

1. ANON. "Designs for First of Famous Americans Stamp Series."
   New York Times (30 December), p. 30:3.
      Illustration of Louisa May Alcott five-cent, "blue" stamp.

1942

2. "Little Women." Collations by D. A. Randall; Notes by J. T.
Winterich. Publishers Weekly, 135 (17 June), 2183-2184.
Describes Little Women first edition and contains brief
anecdote by Alexander Woolcott on book's popularity in Japan.

1940

1. ANON. "First-Day Covers." New York Times, 18 (February), 6:8.
Upon release of Louisa May Alcott stamp, 213,620 first-day
covers were sold.

2. BLANCK, JACOB N. "News from the Rare Book Shops." Publishers
Weekly, 137 (13 January), 154-155.
Recounts variant printings of Little Women in England as
Little Wives and Little Women Wedded.

3. SPENCER, SARA. Little Women, dramatized from Louisa May Alcott's
story. Based on scenario by Robert St. Clair. Anchorage, Ky.:
The Children's Theatre Press.
As the title suggests, a popular dramatization intended for
a juvenile audience.

1941

1. ANON. "Author." New York Times (20 July), VII, p. 14.
Credits Alcott's books with activities which were fore-
runners of modern progressive education.

*2. LEETCH, MARGARET. Reveille in Washington, 1860-1865. New York:
Harper, pp. 222-224, 430.
Listed in Ireland, Index to Women, 1970.3.

1942

1. ADAMS, E. L. "Louisa Alcott's Doomed Manuscript." More Books,
17 (May), 221-222.
Account of recently acquired manuscript letter from Alcott
to publisher James Osgood concerning book manuscript which was
lost twice and finally abandoned.

2. HARDEN, JULIA WOODHOUSE. "Louisa Alcott's Contribution to
Democracy." Negro History Bulletin, 6 (November), 28, 32, 46.
Reveals Miss Alcott's strong antislavery stand, showing the
influence of Garrison, Thoreau, Emerson, Bronson Alcott, and
John Brown.

Writings about Louisa May Alcott

1942

3. HOFFMAN, VIRGINIA M. "Literary Techniques in the Novels of
    Louisa May Alcott." M.A. thesis, University of Iowa.
        Analyzes the literary "spirit and style" which made her
    works endure. Deals with romantic and realistic elements
    then turns to the consideration of Alcott as "reformer and
    moralist." Among literary techniques finds greatest strengths
    in characterization, dialogue, and narrative, which she clas-
    sifies as being written at the level of a child audience.
    Even if they deal with the "plains rather than the peaks of
    experience," these books satisfy Bronson Alcott's wish for
    "better books for children."

4. RUSSELL, FRANK ALDEN. American Pilgrimage. New York: Dodd,
    Mead, pp. 150-164.
        Presents lively if cursory account of Louisa May Alcott's
    life, completely sunny, acknowledging misfortunes of her life
    with somewhat forced good cheer. Same as 1943.4.

1943

1. BLANCK, JACOB N. "News from the Rare Book Sellers; Secret
    Literary Life." Publishers Weekly, 144 (16 October), 1543.
        Describes Stern's "The Witch's Cauldron," pointing out the
    debt to Ms. Rostenberg. Briefly discusses Alcott's work as
    A. M. Barnard.

2. COFFMAN, RAMON PEYTON and NATHAN G. GOODMAN. Famous Authors for
    Boys and Girls. New York: Barnes, pp. 101-106, portrait.
    Same as 1943.3.

3. COFFMAN, RAMON PEYTON and NATHAN G. GOODMAN. Famous Authors for
    Young People. New York: Dodd, Mead, pp. 101-106.
        Recounts childhood events including Bronson's schools,
    Louisa's curiosity, and finally the "room of her own."
    Same as 1943.2.

4. MALONE, TED [pseud. of Frank Alden Russell]. Should Old Acquaint-
    ance. New Jersey: Bookmark, pp. 150-164.
        Same as 1942.4.

5. ROSTENBERG, LEONA. "Some Anonymous and Pseudonymous Thrillers
    of Louisa M. Alcott." Bibliographical Society of America
    Papers, 37 (2nd Quarter), 131-140.
        This first detailed account of Louisa May Alcott's produc-
    tion of sensational "pot-boilers" under pseudonym of A. M.
    Barnard was somewhat limited because the Library of Congress
    had stored the run of The Flag of Our Union for safety during

World War II. It did, however, begin the change in the Alcott image which has been continued by Ms. Rostenberg and Madeleine Stern.

6. STERN, MADELEINE B. "The First Appearance of a 'Little Women' Incident." American Notes and Queries, 3 (October), 99-100.
    Describes Alcott's use of an incident which later appeared in Little Women, not yet finished, while she served as editor of Merry's Museum, January 1868.

7. STERN, MADELEINE B. "Louisa May Alcott: Civil War Nurse." Americana, 37 (April), 296-325.
    Discusses Louisa May Alcott's experiences which resulted in Hospital Sketches. Revived interest in a neglected aspect of Alcott's life.

8. STERN, MADELEINE B. "Louisa M. Alcott's Contributions to Periodicals, 1868-1888." More Books, 18 (1943), 411-420. Reprinted, see 1977.5.
    States that the bulk of Louisa Alcott's writings appeared in periodical literature of the day, many of which are not yet known. Periodical appearances permit study by biographers and bibliographers and reveal many varied techniques. Traces the "career within a career" of writing sensational tales until she "was on the way from the witch's cauldron to the family hearth." Contains a useful appendix listing periodicals, numbers of contributions to each, the years of publication and numbers related to Stern's bibliography in Louisa's Wonder Book: An Unknown Alcott Juvenile.

9. STERN, MADELEINE B. "Louisa Alcott, Trouper; Experiences in Theatricals, 1848-1880." New England Quarterly, (June), pp. 175-197.
    Traces amateur dramatic experiences, using as sources the Journals, playbills, and Whitman correspondence. Maintains that interest in drama shows in all her books, particularly in "homely dialogue" and "skill in heightening a humorous situation." As late as 1880 Alcott dramatized Michael Strogoff "to relive the earlier pleasures of dramatization."

10. STERN, MADELEINE B. "The Witch's Cauldron to the Family Hearth, Louisa M. Alcott's Literary Development, 1848-1868." More Books, 18 (October), 363-380.
    Discusses the early writing of Louisa May Alcott, including melodramas, Flower Fables, "pot-boilers," travel accounts, and finally Work, highly autobiographical and a transition to Little Women.

1943

11. WAGONER, JEAN (BROWN). <u>Louisa Alcott; Girl of Old Boston</u>.
    Indianapolis, New York: Bobbs-Merrill.
    Written with simplicity for young children.

1945

1. NATHAN, GEORGE JEAN. "Little Women." (Review of Marion DeForest
   dramatization.) <u>Theatre Book of the Year: 1944-45</u>,
   pp. 196-197.
   Calls <u>Little Women</u> a "venerable American classic"; defends
   its sentimentality as appropriate and terms play "still ser-
   viceable theatre . . . a felicitous journey out of the hard-
   boiled present into the lace-valentine yesterday."

2. STERN, MADELEINE B. "Louisa M. Alcott's Self Criticism." <u>More
   Books</u>, 20 (October), 339-345.
   Briefly discusses Louisa M. Alcott's analysis of her own
   personal and artistic weaknesses and handicaps.

1946

1. NATHAN, GEORGE JEAN. "Little Women." (Review of Marion DeForest
   dramatization.) <u>Theatre Book of the Year: 1945-46</u>, p. 241.
   Describes 1945 production as slipshod and inferior.

2. VAN DOREN, CARL. <u>The American Novel</u>. New York: Macmillan.
   Contains one reference: Chapter 7, "Howells and Realism."
   States that Louisa M. Alcott and Thomas Bailey Aldrich "turned
   away from the watery illusions which in respectable circles
   had furnished the substance for children's books."

1947

1. MOTT, FRANK LUTHER. <u>Golden Multitudes</u>. New York: Macmillan.
   Provides statistics on sales and position on best-seller
   lists. Calls <u>Little Women</u> the most popular girls' story in
   American literature. Speaks of Alcott's devotion to "The
   Pathetic Family" and of her reactions to Twain and other
   popular writers.

2. SEARS, W. P., JR. "Educational Theories of Louisa May Alcott."
   <u>Dalhousie Review</u>, 27 (October), 327-334.
   After an obviously psychoanalytic debunking of the Alcott
   family myths, discusses the "progressive" educational theories
   evident in major novels. Ends on a confused criticism of
   Alcott's "ordinary" style which has somehow held the interest
   of generations.

1948

1. ANON. <u>The Literary History of the United States</u>. Edited by
    Spiller, Thorp, Johnson, and Canby. New York: Macmillan,
    pp. 383-384.
    Gives the usual bibliographical information to 1948.

2. <u>Oxford Campanion to Literature</u>. Edited by James D. Hart.
    New York: Oxford University Press.
    Lists works only.

1949

1. BOLTON, SARAH K. <u>Lives of Girls Who Became Famous</u>. New York:
    Crowell. Reprint of 1886.3.
    Contains chapter on Louisa May Alcott.

*2. NISENSON, SAMUEL and WILLIAM A. DEWITT. <u>Illustrated Minute</u>
    <u>Biographies</u>. New York: Grosset and Dunlap, p. 11, portrait.
    Listed in Ireland, <u>Index to Women</u>, 1970.3.

3. SALYER, SANDFORD. <u>Marmee/The Mother of Little Women</u>. Norman:
    University of Oklahoma Press.
        Includes many details drawn from <u>Journals</u>. Emphasizes
    influence of Mrs. Alcott on Louisa May as well as reflecting
    her reactions to Alcott's early works. Is based on much un-
    published material, provides new information concerning the
    reception of <u>Moods,</u> and disagrees with Cheney's dating of
    Alcott's stories in <u>The Atlantic Monthly</u>.

4. STERN, MADELEINE B. "Louisa M. Alcott; An Appraisal." <u>New</u>
    <u>England Quarterly</u> (December), pp. 475-498.
        Evaluates <u>Little Women</u>'s greatness based upon universality
    of picture of the American home and its "index of New England
    manners in mid-century." Sensational stories gave Alcott the
    art of emphasis and the ability to heighten the dramatic and
    subordinate the less dramatic. Added use of natural speech
    and knowledge of adolescent psychology.

1950

1. BROOKS, VAN WYCK. <u>New England: Indian Summer. 1865-1915</u>.
    New York: Dutton, pp. 45-65.
        Follows Alcott from Concord to Boston, claiming she forced
    her way into the world ignoring "the conventional notions
    which governed her sex." Sums up Alcott's contribution:

1950

> "She invested the Concord scheme of life with the gaiety and romance of a Robin Hood ballad."

2. COMMAGER, HENRY STEELE. The American Mind. New Haven: Yale University Press.
    Contains no specific mention of Alcott but Commager recognizes her works as a part of "19th century literature's consciousness of childhood" and values Little Women over Elsie Dinsmore--"Little Women had been sentimental but the Elsie books . . . were saccharine."

3. STERN, MADELEINE B. Louisa May Alcott. Norman: University of Oklahoma Press.
    A sound, critical biography, which is in many ways definitive, yet readable. The valuable bibliography and notes on sources provide important scholarly tools.

4. WILSON, CARROLL ATWOOD. Thirteen Author Collections of the Nineteenth Century and Five Centuries of Familiar Quotations. Edited by Jean C. S. Wilson and David A. Randall. Vol. 1. New York: Privately printed for Scribner's, pp. 4-16.
    Includes first editions, also anonymous works such as "Pauline's Passion and Punishment" and "The Mysterious Key and What It Opened." Comments on condition of books in collection.

1951

1. COWIE, ALEXANDER. The Rise of the American Novel. New York: American Book Co., pp. 459, 645, 821.
    Mrs. Stowe's My Wife and I has a wholesome atmosphere comparable to Louisa Alcott and W. D. Howells. Speaks of Twain's crudity: "No wonder Louisa Alcott warned readers against him." Classifies Alcott's stories as "among the better domestic stories." Little Women is not always free of the sentimentalism of contemporary novels but is "blessedly" free of "outworn plot devices" and "morbid elements." Shows genuine humor and truly individualized characters.

2. DEEGAN, DOROTHY. The Stereotype of the Single Woman in American Novels. New York: King's Crown Press.
    Emphasizes Little Women, seeing Jo's struggles for independence as "an excellent commentary upon the place of women in her day."

3. QUINN, ARTHUR HOBSON. The Literature of the American People. New York: Appleton-Century-Crofts.
    Gives a cursory treatment of Louisa May Alcott's popularity.

1952

1. SCHERMAN, DAVID EDWARD. Literary America. New York: Dodd,
    Mead, p. 85.
        Calls Little Women the "book of the year" for 1868. Pic-
    tures attic of Orchard House as happiest spot for Louisa after
    nomadic childhood.

2. WAGENKNECHT, EDWARD. Cavalcade of the American Novel. New York:
    Holt, pp. 88-89, 91.
        Calls Little Women an American David Copperfield, and most
    beloved American book. Describes Little Women as within limits
    of domestic sentimentality, but honest, and even given to
    parody of other contemporary writers.

1953

1. CHESTERTON, G. K. "Louisa Alcott," in A Handful of Authors:
    Essays on Books and Writers. Edited by Dorothy Collins. New
    York: Sheed and Ward, pp. 163-168. Reprint of 1907.2.
        States that he cannot comprehend women and so approached
    Alcott with fear. Surprised to find Alcott books "extremely
    good." Little Women anticipated realism by twenty to thirty
    years, "for women are the only realists." Classes Alcott with
    Jane Austen. Both had "awful womanly irony." Finds details
    "profoundly true"; even from a masculine viewpoint the books
    are good. "From a feminine standpoint they are so good that
    their admirers have really lost sight even of their goodness."
    He retreats but is sure "I leave a very interesting world
    behind me."

2. FAWCETT, CLARA H. "Creative Artists and the Doll: M. Thompson's
    Models of Little Women." Hobbies, 58 (October), 50+.
        Includes photographs of bisque heads of the "Little Women"
    done by Martha Thompson who also dressed them so as to recap-
    ture the spirit of the time of the book. After a brief account
    of the Alcotts and their friends detailed descriptions are
    given of suggested costuming.

3. MEIGS, CORNELIA L., ANN THAXTER EATON, ELIZABETH NESBITT, and
    RUTH HILL VIGUERS. A Critical History of Children's Litera-
    ture. New York: Macmillan, pp. 224-231.
        Under heading "The March Family" relates the bulk of Alcott's
    novels to her life with and for the sake of her family.

*4. MORRIS, RICHARD, ed. Four Hundred Notable Americans. New York:
    Harper and Row, 1953, 1965, p. 22.
        Listed in Ireland, Index to Women, 1970.3.

Writings about Louisa May Alcott

1953

5. "Portrait." <u>Negro History Bulletin</u>, 17 (November), 40.
    Captions picture of Alcott with "anti-slavery sympathizer."

6. STERN, MADELEINE B. "Little Women," in <u>Varied Harvest a Miscel-</u>
    <u>lany of Writing by Barnard College Women</u>. Edited by Amy
    Loveman, Frederica Barsch and Marjorie M. Mayer. New York:
    Putnam, pp. 213-222.
    Excerpt from <u>Louisa May Alcott, see</u> 1950.3.

7. STERN, MADELEINE B. <u>Purple Passage: The Life of Mrs. Frank</u>
    <u>Leslie</u>. Norman: University of Oklahoma Press.
    Contains scattered correspondence and references to
    Alcott's contributions to <u>Frank Leslie's Illustrated Newspaper</u>.

*8. <u>Women on Stamps</u>. Philadelphia Women's Stamp Club (February),
    unpublished pamphlet.
    Cited in Ireland, <u>Index to Women</u>, 1970.3.

1954

1. ANON. "Papers of Great Listed for Study." <u>New York Times</u>
    (17 November), p. 28:4.
    Alcott is one of two dozen women included on list of recom-
    mendations for preservation and publication of personal papers
    of outstanding historical Americans.

2. BOLTON, SARAH K. <u>Famous American Authors</u>. Revised by William A.
    Fahey. New York: Crowell, pp. 159-166. Reprint of 1886.3.

3. LEARY, LEWIS. <u>Articles on American Literature, 1900-1950</u>.
    Durham: Duke University Press, pp. 8-9.
    Brief bibliography. Contains twenty-six entries for
    Louisa May Alcott.

4. PEARE, CATHERINE O. <u>Louisa May Alcott/Her Life</u>. New York:
    Holt.
    Provides a useful study for younger readers. Does not con-
    tribute new materials or concepts. Illustrated by Margaret
    Ayer.

5. STEINBERG, S. H. <u>Cassell's Encyclopedia of World Literature</u>.
    2 vols. New York: Funk and Wagnalls.
    Lists eighteen books by Louisa May Alcott and four biogra-
    phies. Claims that recognition came with publication of
    <u>Hospital Sketches</u> and that Louisa May Alcott produced "real-
    istic portraits and genuine American backgrounds."

6. STERN, MADELEINE B. "Louisa's Wonder Book: A Newly Discovered Alcott Juvenile." <u>American Literature</u>, 26 (November), 384-390.
    Discusses a lost manuscript which appeared anonymously in 1870 as <u>Will's Wonder Book</u>, quite possibly without Miss Alcott's knowledge.

1955

1. BLANCK, JACOB N. "Louisa May Alcott," in <u>Bibliography of American Literature</u>. Vol. 1. New Haven: Yale University Press, pp. 27-45.
    In keeping with stated purpose, lists all first editions chronologically, briefly describes books containing the first appearance of any prose (except letters) or poetry plus variant issues or states of first editions. At the end of the entry gives a selective list of bibliographical, biographical, and critical works.

2. PERÉNYI, ELEANOR. "Dear Louisa." <u>Harper's</u>, 211 (October), 69-72.
    States that source of Alcott's fascination lay in "plain living and high thinking, her liberalism, her charity and breeding, and her "capitalistic conscience." Discusses liberality in attitude toward women's rights and the dignity of labor. Defines Alcott's "modernity" as her mirroring of permanent attitudes inherent in American, especially New England, culture.

1956

1. PAPASHVILY, HELEN WAITE. <u>All the Happy Endings</u>. New York: Harper.
    Briefly examines Alcott's heroines except for those in the earlier, more sensational tales. <u>See</u> 1965.6.

2. PRINGLE, PATRICK. <u>When They Were Girls/Girlhood Stories of Fourteen Famous Women</u>. New York: Roy Publishers, pp. 148-165.
    A selected series of anecdotes, largely derived from Cheney's <u>Journals</u> and from later biographers. Intended for young people.

1957

1. ANON. "Miss Alcott Speaking." <u>New York Times Magazine</u> (24 November), p. 62.
    Contains excerpts from Alcott's writings reflecting scenes, events, and her personality.

1957

2. BARRETT, C. WALLER. "Little Women Forever," in Bibliophile in
    the Nursery. Edited by William Targ. Cleveland: World.
        Brings together little-known facts about the writing and
    publication of Little Women. Traces, through letters and
    journals from 1858 to 1868, Miss Alcott's interest in a
    family chronicle.

3. DUNAWAY, PHILIP and MEL EVANS. A Treasury of the World's Great
    Diaries. New York: Doubleday, pp. 416-418.
        Excerpts ten-year-old Louisa Alcott's diary in section
    titled "Alone, With Other Worlds Outside," suggesting life at
    Fruitlands evoked "gnawing nameless fear" as well as happy
    moments.

4. FENNER, PHYLLIS. The Proof of the Pudding. New York: John Day,
    pp. 133, 188.
        Recounts incidents concerning Little Women readers includ-
    ing observation that boys, inspired by movie, read book with
    brown paper wrappers over cover.

5. HOLBROOK, STEWART HALL. Dreamers of the American Dream. New
    York: Doubleday, pp. 41-42.
        Summarizes brief Fruitlands experience saying Louisa erased
    scars by writing "Transcendental Wild Oats."

6. JAMES, HENRY. "Eight Cousins: or, The Aunt-Hill," in Literary
    Reviews and Essays. Edited by Albert Mordell, New York:
    Twayne, pp. 245-247. Reprint of 1875.4.

7. SCHLESINGER, ELIZABETH BANCROFT. "The Alcotts through Thirty
    Years: Letters to Alfred Whitman." Harvard Library Bulletin
    (11 August), pp. 363-385.
        Contains correspondence of Louisa May, Anna, and Abby May
    Alcott with Whitman, who had spent one year in F. B. Sanborn's
    school and was a friend of the Alcott family. Letters run
    from March 1858 to 29 May 1891 and reveal much of the Alcotts'
    daily life. Concludes that "Louisa, caught in the web of fame,
    tries in vain to find her own soul, while easing the life of
    her beloved family."

1958

1. ANON. Review of Miss Alcott of Concord. Booklist, 55
    (8 September), 183.
        Calls the biography most satisfactory when Worthington
    stays close to Alcott's experiences and writings.

Writing about Louisa May Alcott

Writings about Louisa May Alcott

Writings about Louisa May Alcott

2.   ANON. Review of <u>Miss Alcott of Concord</u>. <u>New Yorker</u>, 34 (18 October), 210.
       Dislikes author's speculations about romances. Calls Alcott "the most widely read transcendentalist today."

3.   ANON. Review of <u>Miss Alcott of Concord</u>. <u>Saturday Review</u>, 41 (October), 170.
       Merely summarizes contents.

4.   ANON. Review of <u>Miss Alcott of Concord</u>. <u>Wisconsin Library Bulletin</u>, 54 (November), 519.
       Calls the book "authentic" but without new insights. The chief revelation is that "Miss Alcott's life was dull."

5.   ESTEROW, MILTON. "TV Put in a Dither by 'Little Women.'" <u>New York Times</u> (31 August), p. 44:3.
       Description of preperformance chaos, especially centering around permitting Beth to live.

6.   HOUGH, HENRY BEETLE. "Micawbers of Massachusetts." <u>Saturday Review</u>, 41 (18 October), 17.
       Reviews <u>Miss Alcott of Concord</u> claiming it follows Alcott's journals closely, yet without offering any interpretive views by biographer.

7.   MAGILL, FRANK N. <u>Cyclopedia of World Authors</u>. New York: Harper.
       Contains standard brief entry calling <u>Little Women</u> "chief claim to fame" of this "ardent abolitionist and advocate of women's suffrage."

8.   SASSCIER, AGNES L. "Collector's Dream Come True, The Alcotts." <u>Hobbies</u>, 63 (April), 106–107+.
       Combines usual biographical material with personal details of collecting first editions of Alcott works.

9.   SMITH, GROVER. "The Doll Burners: D. H. Lawrence and Louisa Alcott." <u>Modern Language Quarterly</u>, 19 (March), 28–32.
       Centers around the doll-burning scene in <u>Little Men</u>. Author finds a clear parallel in <u>Sons and Lovers</u> in which a doll belonging to Paul's sister is burned. Finds that Alcott used the scene to moralize against destructiveness; Lawrence used it as "male retaliation against female domestic ascendancy."

10. THARP, LOUISE HALL. "Miss Minerva Moody." Review of <u>Miss Alcott of Concord</u>. <u>New York Times Book Review</u>, (19 October), 30:4.

Writings about Louisa May Alcott

1958

> Generally favorable review of Worthington's biography. Criticizes Cheney's "suppression" of the "real" Miss Alcott.

11. WALBRIDGE, E. F. Review of Miss Alcott of Concord. Library Journal, 83 (15 September), 2438.
     Resents insertion of the author's own experiences. Greatest value lies in a previously unpublished letter commenting on the Hawthornes.

12. WORTHINGTON, MARJORIE. Miss Alcott of Concord/A Biography. New York: Doubleday.
     Reworks material from Cheney's edition, adding the author's own experience. Contains a previously unpublished letter commenting on the Hawthornes.

1959

1. YOUNG, AGATHA. The Women and the Crisis: Women of the North in the Civil War. New York: McDowell, Obolensky, pp. 228-232.
    Interesting juxtaposition with Walt Whitman. Alcott's Hospital Sketches are classed with The Wound Dresser. Describes Alcott's introduction to hospital nursing, her illness, and the effect of the experience upon her writing. Feels that it gave "richer maturity" and that "life for her was never the same again."

1960

1. CARPENTER, NAN COOKE. "Louisa May Alcott and Thoreau's Flute." Huntington Library Quarterly, 24 (November), 71-74.
    Reviews the writing of "Thoreau's Flute"; reproduces diary entries concerning the poem, and reprints two letters from Alcott treating Mrs. Hawthorne's sponsorship and Fields's acceptance.

2. PEATTIE, DONALD and LOUISE. "Louisa May Alcott. Greatest of 'Little Women.'" Reader's Digest, 74 (June), 256-264.
    A popular treatment of the burdens which Alcott assumed as the "man" of the family. Illustrates the hold which Little Women has on the American public by the flood of protests resulting when the 1958 TV version did not include the death of Beth. Notes the ironic contrast between the financial rewards from movies and TV and the bitter poverty of the Alcotts. Classifies Little Women as a true novel "constructed with masterly craft and honesty."

Writings about Louisa May Alcott

3. STEEGMULLER, FRANCIS. "House of Little Women." <u>Holiday</u>, 27 (March), 158, 191-192.
       An interesting, detailed description of Orchard House in Concord. Individual rooms are related to the characters in <u>Little Women</u>. Testimony to the vivid reality of the novel is provided by the account of the disappointment felt by many visiting children when they learn that there never was a Laurence mansion next door, the house which figures so largely in the stories of Laurie and his grandfather. The account closes: "It is astonishing, both in the pages of the book and in the rooms of old Orchard House, how very alive they still are."

1961

1. FISHER, MARGERY. <u>Intent upon Reading</u>. New York: Watts, pp. 297-298.
       Calls Alcott tales nearer to reality, giving children more truth than modern books do.

2. GERSTENBERGER, DONNA and GEORGE HENDRICK. <u>The American Novel 1789-1959/A Checklist of Twentieth Century Criticism</u>. Denver: Alan Swallow, pp. 8-9.
       Contains twelve bibliographical items, unfortunately not those of the centennial year for <u>Little Women</u>, 1968.

1962

1. BROWNING, DAVID C., ed. <u>Everyman's Dictionary of Literary Biography: English and American</u>. Revised edition. New York: Dutton.
       Credits "guidance in her education" to Thoreau and Emerson. Briefly traces life and career.

2. MEIGS, CORNELIA L. "Running in the Wind," in <u>Roads to Greatness</u>. Edited by Louise Galloway. New York: Crowell-Collier Publishing Company, pp. 344-370.
       Selection from <u>Invincible Louisa</u> describing the Fruitlands experience, the saving of the family unity, and the years in Concord until Alcott was sixteen.

3. SPILLER, ROBERT. <u>Literary History of the United States</u>. New York: Macmillan, pp. 383-384. Also <u>Supplement</u>, p. 75.
       Updated bibliographical list.

1963

1. DOLAN, JOSEPHINE A. <u>Goodnow's History of Nursing</u>. 11th edition.
    Philadelphia: W. B. Saunders, p. 236.
    Quotes from <u>Hospital Sketches</u> as evidence of Alcott's
    "common sense" approach to nursing, as well as her opposition
    to overworking nurses, or using still weak convalescents.

1964

1. BLIVEN, BRUCE. "Mama, They've Begun Again." <u>American Heritage</u>,
    16 (December), 12-16+.
    Credits Louisa with providing happiness and security for
    her father, Bronson, the agreeable but totally improvidential
    philosopher.

2. BROPHY, BRIGID. "Sentimentality and Louisa M. Alcott." <u>Sunday</u>
    <u>Times Magazine</u> (December). Reprinted, see 1965.3.
    Explores the mystery of why <u>Little Women</u> still lives and
    concludes that despite the sentimentality which appeals to
    the "lowbrow" there is technical skill which attracts the
    "highbrow." Traces this skill to the differentiation of the
    March girls, especially Jo, "one of the most blatantly auto-
    biographical yet most fairly treated heroines in print." Sees
    such craftmanship in sentimentality making possible enjoyment
    of this genre, at first described as "dreadful."

*3. STILES, KENT B. <u>Postal Saints and Sinners</u>. Theo. Gans' Sons,
    p. 6.
    Listed in Ireland, <u>Index to Women</u>, 1970.3.

1965

1. ANON. Review of Papashvily's <u>Louisa May Alcott</u>. <u>Library Journal</u>,
    90 (July), 3127.
    Classifies the biography as falling in age appeal between
    the biography by Catherine Peare (1954) and "the distinguished
    <u>Invincible Louisa</u> by Cornelia Meigs."

2. BLANCK, JACOB N. <u>Merle Johnson's American First Editions</u>. 4th
    edition. Waltham, Mass.: Mark Press, pp. 12-15.
    Includes a bibliography of Alcott first editions.

3. BROPHY, BRIGID. "Sentimentality and Louisa M. Alcott." <u>New York</u>
    <u>Times Book Review</u> (17 January), pp. 1, 44. Reprint of 1964.2.
    Also listed as "A Masterpiece, and Dreadful."

4. HUBER, MIRIAM BLANTON. Story and Verse for Children. 3rd edi-
    tion. New York: Macmillan.
        Calls Alcott family "cultured but improvident"; terms
    Little Women "loved" by boys and girls.

5. "Letters to the Editor." New York Times Book Review
    (7 February), p. 34:3.
        Assorted reactions to 1965.3.

6. PAPASHVILY, HELEN WAITE. Louisa May Alcott. Boston: Houghton
    Mifflin.
        Expansion of material used in 1956.1, into a biography
    making use of letters, diaries, and other primary materials.

7. TAYLOR, MILLICENT. Review of Papashvily's Louisa May Alcott.
    Christian Science Monitor (4 November).
        Despite use of the usual early materials, displays "under-
    standing of Miss Alcott's deep tempestuous character."

1966

1. DAVIS, DOROTHY R. The Carolyn Sherwin Bailey Historical Collec-
    tion of Children's Books. A catalogue. Southern Connecticut
    State College, p. 18.
        Lists Alcott volumes in the Bailey collection.

2. DOUGLAS, EMILY TAFT. Remember the Ladies. New York: Putnam,
    p. 144.
        Briefly quotes Alcott's description of Georgetown hospital;
    recounts that she, like a "sensible girl," was soon scrubbing
    away despite her initial shock.

3. HAVILAND, VIRGINIA, comp. Children's Literature/A Guide to
    Reference Sources. Washington: Library of Congress,
    pp. 66-67.
        Contains annotations on works by Cheney (1928), Gulliver
    (1932), Meigs (1933), Stern (1943 and 1950). The selection
    is intended for children and adolescents.

1967

1. BEACH, SETH CURTIS. Daughters of the Puritans. Freeport, New
    York: Books for Libraries Press, pp. 251-286. Reprint of
    1905.4.

1967

2. BLANCK, JACOB N. "The Juvenile Reading of Certain Nineteenth-
   Century American Writers." Massachusetts Historical Society
   Proceedings, 79: 64-73.
   Traces the limited and restricted materials available to
   juvenile readers of the nineteenth century. Among those
   treated is Alcott who in her home "unlike any other either
   before or since" was guided by her father to ready widely:
   Byron, Plutarch, Dickens, Martin Luther, Scott, Lydia Maria
   Child, and Goethe, among others. Blanck finds Alcott an ex-
   ception to "those ancestral children" who were deprived of
   "the pleasures of reading."

3. BROPHY, BRIGID. "Sentimentality and Louisa M. Alcott," in
   Don't Never Forget. London: Jonathan Cape; New York: Holt.
   Same as 1964.2 and 1965.3.

4. COAN, OTIS W. and RICHARD G. LILLARD. America in Fiction. 5th
   edition. Palo Alto: Pacific Books.
   Lists Little Women in section on "Farm and Village Life"
   saying it "shows the integrity and virtues of American
   villager."

5. DARLING, RICHARD L. "Authors vs. Critics: Children's Books in
   the 1870's: Excerpt from The Rise of Children's Book Review-
   ing in America, 1865-1881." Publishers Weekly, 192
   (16 October), 25-27.
   Excerpts demonstrate Alcott's criticism of "sensational"
   books for boys and quotes some of William T. Adams acerbic
   reactions.

1968

1. ANON. "Little Women Centennial Celebrated by Little, Brown."
   Library Journal, 93 (15 October), 3916.
   Recounts first publication of Little Women and lists three
   publications for centennial.

2. BRADFORD, GAMALIEL. Portraits and Personalities. Freeport,
   New York: Books for Libraries Press, pp. 133-153. Reprint
   of 1933.4.

3. DOYLE, BRIAN. The Who's Who of Children's Literature. New York:
   Schocken Books, pp. 4-5.
   Calls Little Women "most popular and widely-read book ever
   written for girls." Includes brief biographical sketch, portrait (fp. 157) and listing of her other books.

4. FISHER, AILEEN and OLIVE RABE. <u>We Alcotts/The Story of Louisa M.</u>
   <u>Alcott's Family as Seen through the Eyes of "Marmee," Mother</u>
   <u>of Little Women</u>. New York: Atheneum.
      This centennial publication provides a new approach as the
   point of view character is Mrs. Alcott.

5. FISHER, AILEEN and OLIVE RABE. "Writing about the Alcotts."
   <u>Horn Book</u>, 44 (October), pp. 541-544.
      Describes the techniques involved in the creation of
   1968.4.

6. GOULD, JACK. "T. V.: The March Sisters." <u>New York Times</u>
   (17 October), p. 59:4.
      Generally negative review of musical treatment of <u>Little</u>
   <u>Women</u>, as fragmentary, indecisive, and generally poorly cast.

7. HAVERSTICK, IOLA. "To See Louisa Plain." <u>Saturday Review</u>, 51
   (19 October), 35+.
      Commends Alcott's growth as writer, as well as courage and
   determination to provide financial support for family. Suggests she enjoyed writing sensational stories even more than
   juveniles.

8. HEINS, PAUL. Review of <u>We Alcotts</u>. <u>Horn Book</u>, 44 (October), 540.
      A generally favorable review.

9. JANEWAY, ELIZABETH. "Meg, Jo, Beth and Amy." <u>New York Times</u>
   <u>Book Review</u> (29 September), pp. 42-46.
      Judges <u>Little Women</u> to be "compulsively readable because
   it is <u>about</u> life and life that is recognizable in human terms
   today." Sees "Jo" and her creator as "New Woman capable of
   male virtues but not . . . unsexed." Finds <u>Invincible Louisa</u>
   still valuable for its reflection of New England culture and
   the internal and external life of Miss Alcott. Does not feel
   that use of Mrs. Alcott as point of view character in <u>We</u>
   <u>Alcotts</u> added much to the study. Records amazement at the
   sentimentality and Victorian conventionalities in the stories
   in Meigs's <u>Glimpses of Louisa</u> and subsequent amazement at the
   timelessness and vitality of <u>Little Women</u>.

10. KELLER, JOHN. Editorial to Centenary Edition. <u>Horn Book</u>, 44
    (October), 519.
       Discussion of <u>Little Women</u> and its subsequent impact.

11. "Letters." <u>New York Times Book Review</u> (3 November), p. 56:3.
       Readers various replies to Janeway article and Mrs.
    Janeway's answer. Correspondence hinges on the question
    of women.

1968

12. MEIGS, CORNELIA L., ed. Glimpses of Louisa/A Centennial Sampling
    of the Best Short Stories by Louisa May Alcott. Boston:
    Little, Brown.
        Editor intends her selection of short stories to afford
    new glimpses of Miss Alcott because of the autobiographical
    coloring of all of the author's work.

13. MEIGS, CORNELIA L. "Introduction," in Little Women, Centennial
    Edition. Boston: Little, Brown.
        Presents an important distillation of Meigs's critical
    judgment of Alcott. Louisa May Alcott's strength lay in her
    honesty, awareness of the danger of overmoralizing, and in
    her ability to present a story with a distinctive pattern and
    an atmosphere in which there appears "splendor in the unfold-
    ing of every person's life, its joy or pain or despair."
    Concludes that Louisa's counterpart in Pilgrim's Progress,
    from which chapter headings came, had to be Mr. Valiant-for-
    truth.

14. MEIGS, CORNELIA L. "Introduction to Glimpses of Louisa." Horn
    Book, 44 (October), 545-549.
        Condenses introduction to 1968.12.

15. MEIGS, CORNELIA L. "Introduction to the Centennial Edition of
    Little Women." Horn Book, 44 (October), 527-535. Reprint of
    1968.14.

16. MEIGS, CORNELIA L. Invincible Louisa. Boston: Little, Brown.
    Reprint of 1933.7.

17. MEIGS, CORNELIA L. Three introductions to Alcott stories. Horn
    Book, 44 (October).
        "Introduction" to Alcott Centennial Edition of Invincible
    Louisa, 536-39, "Introduction" to Glimpses of Louisa, 545-49,
    and "Introduction" to the centennial edition of Little Women,
    527-535. In the last, Meigs reemphasizes that Louisa May
    Alcott "came to the mastery of her art by living rather than
    by writing."

18. O'FAOLAIN, SEAN. "This is Your Life: Louisa May Alcott."
    Holiday, 44 (November), 18-26.
        Claims that Alcott "exorcised her miserable past" by
    "fibbing" about the "gaiety and gusto" of the March (Alcott)
    household in Little Women. Calls period "least attractive"
    in American history, but praises Alcott's glimpses of hard
    reality. Recalls her early efforts under pen name of Flora
    Fairfield. Suggests key to reticences is omission of father
    and "watering down of bitter wine of actual poverty."

19. RUSS, LAVINIA. "I Want to Do Something Splendid." <u>Publishers Weekly</u>, 194 (2 September), 29-31.
    Records centennial publication of three Alcott books. Quotes extensively from Meigs's introduction to <u>Invincible Louisa</u>, which notes Alcott's tremendous struggle against "snubs and slights and the unfair exploitation" as she earned her independence.

20. RUSS, LAVINIA. "Not To Be Read on Sunday." <u>Horn Book</u>, 44 (October), 521-526.
    Once again probes the appeal of <u>Little Women</u> in an age of violence and challenges such negative critics as Brigid Brophy. Sees Louisa as a rebel, the child of constructive rebels, whose faith in their ability to accept the responsibility for changing the world appeals to young people in 1968. Title is taken from an early review that stated <u>Little Women</u> is not a religious book and therefore "not to be read on Sunday."

<u>1969</u>

1. FOLEY, P. K. <u>American Authors, 1795-1895</u>. New York: Milford House, pp. 3-5.
   Listing of works does not include the pseudonymous and anonymous "pot-boilers."

2. GOULD, JACK. "T. V. Little Women Dance." <u>New York Times</u> (26 May), p. 95:3.
   Critical review of interpretations of scenes from <u>Little Women</u> by Children's Ballet Theater: too much narrative, too little dancing.

3. JANEWAY, ELIZABETH. "Meg, Jo, Beth, Amy and Louisa," in Sheila Egoff, et al. <u>Only Connect; Readings in Children's Literature</u>. New York: Oxford, pp. 286-290.
   Admits deficiencies of <u>Little Women</u> as accused by Brophy and others, but calls Alcott's portraits of girls "clear, unequivocal, and humanly right." Claims continuing popularity of books rests in Jo--the only nineteenth-century heroine who fulfills timeless "dream of growing up into full humanity rather than limited femininity."

4. MEIGS, CORNELIA L., et al. <u>A Critical History of Children's Literature</u>. New York: Macmillan, pp. 207-214.
   In a section, "The American Family," the March family is used as the base for discussion of Louisa May Alcott who "cannot be considered apart from her family." Consequently over half of the entry is devoted to biographical details, the

1969

remainder to bibliographical facts, ending with a tribute to Louisa May because she "opened a door through which thousands of readers all over the world are still passing to share the life of an ideal home with its moral earnestness, innate refinement, and its liberality of thought."

5. ULLOM, JUDITH C. Louisa May Alcott/A Centennial for "Little Women." Washington: Library of Congress.
    Prepared by Children's Book Section to serve in part as a catalog of the exhibit of Alcott items to celebrate the centennial of Little Women (3 October 1868). Foreword indicates materials included and their arrangement by series or type rather than chronology. Contains illustrations from first editions and selections from prefaces and contemporary reviews. Restores Alcott's position in the history of the domestic novel without reducing her stature in children's literature.

1970

1. COHN, JAN. "The Negro Character in Northern Magazine Fiction of the 1860's." New England Quarterly, 43: 572-592.
    Studies survival of some of stereotypes of northern abolitionists and southern slaveholders in stories of Louisa May Alcott, among others.

2. HAMBLEN, ABIGAIL A. "Louisa May Alcott and the 'Revolution' in Education." Journal of General Education, 22: 81-92.
    Discusses Bronson Alcott's theories on education, which emphasized educating the whole child, stressing physical education and hygiene, and educating girls as well as boys to become socially aware individuals. In the books of the Little Women series, Alcott dramatizes these educational concepts of her father.

3. IRELAND, NORMA OLIN. Index to Women of the World from Ancient to Modern Times. Westwood, Mass.: F. W. Faxon, p. 9.
    Contains thirty-six entries on Louisa May Alcott. Indexes 945 books and collections to 1968.

4. KELLY, ROBERT GORDON. "Mother Was a Lady; Strategy and Order in Selected American Children's Periodicals, 1865-1890." Ph.D. dissertation, University of Iowa.
    Examines domestic fiction found in St. Nicholas, Youth's Companion, Wide Awake, Our Young Folks, and Riverside Magazine for Young People. Sees use of periodicals to enforce cultural concepts and mores. See 1974.4.

5. LEARY, LEWIS. <u>Articles on American Literature, 1950-1967</u>.
    Durham, N.C.: Duke University Press.
        Contains eight entries for Louisa May Alcott.

6. LEVY, DAVID W. "Racial Stereotypes in Anti-Slavery Fiction."
    <u>Phylon</u>, 31 (Fall), 265-279.
        Finds works by H. B. Stowe, L. M. Alcott, R. Hildreth,
    John Trawbridge "riddled by the kind of racial stereotypes
    common in pro-slavery fiction."

7. PICKETT, LASALLE (CORBELL). "Louisa May Alcott," in <u>Across My
    Path, Memories of People I Have Known</u>. Freeport, New York:
    Books for Libraries Press, pp. 105-111. Reprint of 1916.1.
        After customary accolade, devotes much time to conversation
    in which Alcott denied that <u>Little Women</u> was her "true" style
    and claimed that she would write in "a lurid style" if it were
    not for "the proper grayness of Concord" and the shock felt by
    Mr. Emerson and her father. Alcott felt, "I shall always be
    a wretched victim to the respectable traditions of Concord."

                            <u>1971</u>

1. CROMPTON, MARGARET. "Little Women: The Making of a Classic."
    <u>Contemporary Review</u>, 218 (February), 99-104.
        Contains a concise history of Alcott family, emphasizing
    Louisa's commitment to provide for their support in lieu of
    idealistic yet ineffectual father, Bronson. Calls Louisa
    "firm realist" who "valued her independence."

2. EICHELBERGER, CLAYTON L. <u>United States Fiction, 1870-1910</u>.
    Metuchen, N.J.: Scarecrow Press.
        Bibliography of criticism in periodicals, 1870-1910. Con-
    tains thirty-nine Louisa May Alcott entries listed according
    to work reviewed.

3. HAMBLEN, ABIGAIL A. "Louisa May Alcott and the Racial Question."
    <u>New Letters</u>, 37 (Summer), 307-313.
        Recounts events and influences which made Alcott an aboli-
    tionist. Traces her journal entries on race as well as plots
    of stories concerned with topic--"M. L." and "My Contraband"
    ("The Brothers"). Calls Alcott's views on miscegenation "para-
    doxical" since she retained strong feelings of "class conscious-
    ness and superiority to other minorities."

4. KIRKLAND, WINIFRED and FRANCES. "Louisa Alcott, The Girl Who
    Wrote for Girls," in <u>Girls Who Became Writers</u>. Freeport, New
    York: Books for Libraries Press, pp. 92-102.

1971

Sees Alcott as remaining a girl at heart. Brief biography which makes use of Alcott journals. Adds little new, limited in scope.

5. SMITH, DAVID E. "Louisa May Alcott," in Notable American Women 1607-1950. Vol. 1. Edited by Edward T. James, et. al. Cambridge, Mass.: Belknap, pp. 27-31.
    A concise, detailed presentation of Alcott's life devoted to "charming and straight forward pictures of nineteenth-century domesticity, seen through the sensibility of the virginal adolescent girl of the day." She presented the "American home with its teapots and curtains, its centripetal and protective femininity" with "the vividness and detail of a Currier and Ives print." Smith feels that Little Women "defined once and for all the values of the American middle-class home of that period." This may explain the lasting charm of the book.

6. STERN, MADELEINE B. Louisa May Alcott. 2nd printing. Norman: University of Oklahoma Press.
    Brings bibliography to date with final list numbering 274, including all known poems, essays, stories, and novels, chrono-logically arranged. Includes reprints and later collections and the sensational and sentimental stories published under pseudonyms.
    Note: Most manuscript material listed in "Notes on Sources" as being deposited at Orchard House is now in the Houghton Library. See 1950.3.

7. WARD, MARTHA E. and DOROTHY A. MARQUARDT. Authors of Books for Young Children. 1st supplement. Metuchen, N.J.: Scarecrow Press, p. 8.
    Lists juvenile novels only.

1972

1. FENWICK, SARA INNIS. "American Children's Classics: Which Will Fade, Which Endure." Wilson Library Bulletin, 47 (October), 178-185.
    Accords Little Women position as one of four books which established field of distinctive modern literature for chil-dren. Calls Little Women most continuously read novel but suggests that sequel, Little Men, is disappointing to modern readers.

2. SALWONCHIK, MARIE. "The Educational Ideas of Louisa May Alcott." Ph.D. dissertation, Loyola University of Chicago.

Examines educational implications found in <u>Little Women</u>, <u>Little Men</u>, and <u>Jo's Boys</u> with special attention to New England transcendentalism, women's rights, and personal and social relevance.

3. SPACKS, PATRICIA MEYER. "Taking Care: Some Women Novelists." <u>Novel</u>, 6 (Fall), 36-51.
    Studies novels of late nineteenth and early twentieth centuries which display "feminine consciousness of the cost of happy marriage with its focus on 'taking care.'" <u>Women's Studies Abstracts</u>, 2 (Spring 1973), 59.

1973

1. HARRINGTON, STEPHANIE. "Does 'Little Women' Belittle Women?" <u>New York Times</u>, 10 (June), II, p. 19.
    Regards <u>Little Women</u> as virtually "a feminist tract," as being presented on TV and as contrasted to other shows. To modern women it seems outdated but it is true to its age and the women characters are "liberated" for the time.

2. LERMAN, LEO. "Little Women/Who's in Love with Miss Louisa May Alcott? I Am." <u>Mademoiselle</u>. (December)
    A Christmas tribute to his "love affair" with Louisa May, one lasting throughout his life. Alcott, for him, represents the promise, the hope, the optimism of America. Finds the book as immediate as a snapshot: "It is living by people over one hundred years ago and, miracle of miracles, clear for us to see, to feel, to smell and to taste because a New England spinster lady had the genius and the wit and the ambition and the need to write it all down."

3. PAYNE, ALMA J. "Duty's Child: Louisa May Alcott." <u>American Literary Realism</u>, 6, no. 3 (Summer), 260-261. In M.L.A. Seminar, "The Celebration and Degradation of Women in Late 19th Century American Fiction," pp. 255-261.
    Traces the development of the sense of duty to her family from Amos Bronson Alcott's prophetic description of Louisa as "Duty's Faithful Child." Briefly describes the conflict between her natural individuality and the constantly reinforced centrality of the Alcott family. Includes other duties: to artistic integrity, to her image as liberated woman, and to various reforms.

4. PAYNE, ALMA J. "Louisa May Alcott (1832-1888)." <u>American Literary Realism</u>, 6, no. 1 (Winter), 27-45.

1973

In-depth bibliographic essay traces history of Alcott criticism; evaluates bibliographic sources; reviews editions, reprints, and published manuscript material; notes manuscript collections and current critical articles (1960-1973); and closes with a discussion of areas of potential future scholarship. Among the latter are lesser-known Alcott novels, Alcott as New Woman, dramas, and Alcott as sociocultural mirror.

5. ROOT, SHELDON L., JR. and NCTE. Adventuring with Books. New York: Citation Press, p. 77.
   Lists Little Women under heading of historical fiction of United States. Calls it "cherished story" with "strong characterizations." Recommends Little Men as well.

1974

1. DIAMONT, SARAH ELBERT. "Louisa May Alcott and the Woman Problem." Ph.D. dissertation, Cornell University.
   Emphasizes Alcott's commitment to both domestic reform and women's rights movements. Sees tensions in both works and life as resulting in her criticism of the dominant materialistic values.

2. FORREY, CAROLYN. "The New Woman Revisited." Women's Studies, no. 2, pp. 37-56.
   Describes "New Woman" of the 1890s in America as "an ideal, an image of self-reliancy and independence including perhaps financial independence and living alone." Includes Alcott's Jo's Boys among others. Women's Studies Abstracts, 3 (Fall), 65.

3. GAY, CAROL. "The Philosopher and His Daughter: Amos Bronson Alcott and Louisa." Essays in Literature (Western Illinois University), no. 2, pp. 181-191.
   Suggests that Louisa Alcott never understood or respected her "controversial father," with all his "potential humbug." Rather, she was "driven by a blind desire to please him and by her own intellectual and psychological limitations; she succeeded in giving him what he neither desired nor needed." M.L.A. Abstracts, 1971, p. 174.

4. KELLY, ROBERT GORDON. Mother Was a Lady/Self and Society in Selected American Children's Periodicals, 1865-1890. Westport, Conn.: Greenwood Press, passim.
   Includes numerous references to Alcott in the discussion of images projected in popular American periodicals for children. See 1970.4.

70

1975

5. MOORE, KATHARINE. <u>Victorian Wives</u>. New York: St. Martin's,
    pp. 191-196.
        Denies Abba Alcott's resemblance to "Marmee," suggesting
    her children suffered from her impractical philanthropy.
    Louisa especially bore financial responsibility for mother's
    comfort in later life. Moore suggests such pressures from
    Abba resulted in Louisa's work excesses and frequent
    breakdowns.

6. MOSS, HOWARD. "Instant Lives: Excerpts." <u>Vogue</u>, 163 (May), 42.
        Amusing "take-off" on the Alcott sisters, here named Louisa,
    Karen, Lupe, and Olga--all uneducated, all suspect in the eyes
    of Concord. It is Concord that is really the target from the
    postmaster, Mr. Crockett, who would "rather spend the day with
    [his] hamster than a night with the Alcott girls," to
    Mrs. Fortress-Rondeau, the town's censor, who had condemned
    <u>Little Men</u> as "a vile pit of unseemliness for minds under
    twelve and a jungle of ugly sensuality for those thirteen
    and over." Amusing illustration.

<u>1975</u>

1. BANNON, BARBARA A. "Story behind the Book: <u>Behind a Mask:</u>
   <u>The Unknown Thrillers of Louisa May Alcott</u>." <u>Publishers</u>
   <u>Weekly</u>, 207 (20 June), 40.
        Provides account of Stern and Rostenberg discovery of
    "thrillers" written by Alcott in early career.

2. BEDELL, MADELON. "Forward: Why Miss Alcott Turned Her Pen to
    the Lurid Style." <u>Redbook</u>, 146 (December), 149-150.
        Precedes reprint of "Behind a Mask." Calls work "anti-
    Gothic" with villainous heroine but one of Alcott's best
    efforts. Highlights Alcott's feminist rebelliousness and
    pragmatic approach to her writing.

3. GLEASON, GENE. "Whatever Happened to Oliver Optic." <u>Wilson</u>
    <u>Library Bulletin</u>, 49 (May), 647-650.
        Recounts Alcott's quarrel with William T. Adams, whose
    books she accused of being too slangy and too interested in
    crime and deviousness. Records Adams's attack on her for
    reading his works "with her elbows."

4. MEERS, ELLEN. "Denaro, lavoro e piccalo donne: Il realismo
    femminile." <u>Communita</u>, 30: 179-205.
    _____. "Money, the Job and Little Women." <u>Commentary</u>, 55
    (January 1973), 57-65.

1975

Reveals "feminine tradition of concern for economic life
of women" in works of Austin, Bronte, Stowe and Alcott.
Women's Studies Abstracts, 2 (Spring 1973), 58.

5. PAULY, THOMAS H. "Ragged Dick and Little Women: Idealized Homes
    and Unwanted Marriages." Journal of Popular Culture, 9
    (Winter), 583-592.
       Compares two novels written for boys or girls exclusively.
    Suggests that both books depicted essentially fatherless
    households, thus undermining marriage while seeming to
    celebrate it.

6. SHULL, MARTHA IRENE. "The Novels of Louisa May Alcott as Com-
    mentary on the American Family." Ph.D. dissertation, Bowling
    Green State University.
       Describes family system in Alcott novels as matriarchal,
    yet conservative in preservation of family patterns. Suggests
    that generations of Alcott readers have shaped modern family
    myths.

7. STERN, MADELEINE B. Louisa's Wonder Book: An Unknown Alcott
    Juvenile. Introduction and bibliography by Stern. Mount
    Pleasant: Central Michigan University.
       Contains nineteen-page introduction tracing the varied
    mishaps the original manuscript went through before finally
    being published serially in Merry's Museum and later in a
    four-volume set, The Dirigo Series. Bibliography, 25-52.

8. TOWNSEND, JOHN ROWE. Written for Children: An Outline of
    English-language Children's Literature. Philadelphia and
    New York: J. B. Lippincott, pp. 78-80.
       Condescending treatment of Alcott's life and work which
    "have been written about endlessly." Does see Little Women
    as ending the "stiff and authoritarian stereotype of family
    life." It opened the door to the family story revealing
    "mutual affection."

1976

1. ANON. Review of Trudel's Siege. Center for Children's Books
    Bulletin, 30 (September), 1.
       Claims names of characters, originally German, were changed
    to Dutch to fit the setting. Calls Trudel "typical Victorian
    heroine: loving, pious, industrious, honest." Finds story
    "sticky-sweet" but "of interest to Alcott fans." Terms
    illustrations "cluttered" and "unconvincing."

1976

2. ANON. Review of <u>Trudel's Siege</u>. <u>Kirkus Reviews</u>, 44 (15 July),
   794.
        Calls story sentimental and undistinguished; suggests it
   did not deserve reissue.

3. ANON. Review of <u>Trudel's Siege</u>. <u>Publishers Weekly</u>, 210
   (2 August), 113.
        Calls Stan Sardinski's illustrations of this reprint of
   story from <u>Lulu's Library</u> appropriate and appealing. Claims
   story "a bit saccharine for modern tastes" but terms Alcott
   "the master storyteller."

4. AUERBACH, NINA. "Austen and Alcott on Matriarchy: New Women or
   New Wives?" <u>Novel</u>, 10 (Fall), 6-26. Reprinted, <u>see</u> 1977.1.
        Characterizes the two novels, <u>Pride and Prejudice</u> and <u>Little
   Women</u> as representing matriarchal families, but claims the
   Alcott novel presents the microcosm as rich and full, convey-
   ing especially the "primary reality of physical things."

5. GAMBLE, MICHAEL W. "The Traveling Plays of Clare Tree Major."
   Paper presented at the Annual Meeting of the American Theatre
   Association (Los Angeles, August) ERIC. ED 126545, C 5501458.
        Analyzes script of "Little Women" for Major's philosophy
   in selection and adaptation of children's stories.

6. "Louisa May Alcott on the Concord Centennial." <u>Women's Studies
   Newsletter</u>, 4 (Fall), 12-13.
        Reprints Alcott report of women's participation in Concord
   centennial celebration which originally appeared in <u>The
   Woman's Journal</u>, 1 May 1875. Subtitled "Unofficial Incidents
   Overlooked by Reporters," Alcott records indignities suffered
   by those women who wished to hear speeches.

7. MCCURRY, NIKI ALPERT. "Concepts of Childrearing and Schooling
   in the March Novels of Louisa May Alcott." Ph.D. dissertation,
   Northwestern University.
        Claims that Alcott's ideas about education and woman's role
   became "increasingly her own" as March novels developed,
   despite sharing father's image of education as spiritual
   pilgrimage.

8. MONTIERO, GEORGE. "Louisa May Alcott's Proverb Stories."
   <u>Tennessee Folklore Society Bulletin</u>, 42 (September), 103-107.
        Calls stories uncommon examples of epigraphic use of
   proverbs, as well as source of liberal examples of regional
   folk-speech, of which thirty are listed.

Writings about Louisa May Alcott

1977

1. AUERBACH, NINA. "Austen and Alcott on Matriarchy: New Women or
   New Wives," in Towards a Poetics of Fiction. Edited by Mark
   Spilka. Indiana University Press, pp. 266-286. Reprint of
   1976.4.

2. ELLIS, KATE. "Life with Marmee: Three Versions," in The Classic
   American Novel and the Movies. Edited by Gerald Peary and
   Roger Shatzkin. New York: Ungar, pp. 62-72. (Film versions
   of Little Women.)
   Compares 1933 and 1949 film treatments with the novel Little
   Women. Sees the book as modifying the Puritan family pattern
   by the presentation of self-sufficient women in an age when
   the feminist movement was growing. States that the working
   woman was out of fashion in 1933 and 1949. Complexity of Jo's
   character escapes Hollywood. 1949 film erases generation gap
   in a growing Hollywood emphasis on youth.

3. GAMBLE, MICHAEL W. "An Analysis of the Playwriting Techniques
   of Clare Tree Major." Children's Theatre Review, 26, no. 1:
   2-4.
   Discusses Clare Tree Major's adaptation of classic children's literature into drama, especially Louisa May Alcott's
   Little Women.

4. SAXTON, MARTHA. Louisa May: A Modern Biography of Louisa May
   Alcott. Boston: Houghton Mifflin.
   Modernity lies in the interpretation of various themes
   often repeated in earlier biographies. Alcott's search for
   a reliable ethic resulted in four values in Little Women:
   good and bad, male and female. Louisa's "sullen vaporous"
   rage became the "guilty center of her life." Louisa feared
   and distrusted men, indulged in writing pseudonymous gothics
   "as if it were a carnal act." Alcott abandoned this genre
   for Little Women which "was a regression for Louisa as artist
   and woman" and a "reversion to adolescent morality." Alcott
   stopped growing; she was unable ro rise above her experience
   and heredity, although she became an active, contributing
   member of society. "She paid a great price in loneliness";
   although her father's quest for perfection gave Louisa a
   sense of "worthlessness and depravity" she eventually made
   a kind of peace with herself and, ironically, she achieved
   the success which he had sought.

5. STERN, MADELEINE B. "Louisa M. Alcott in Periodicals." Studies
   in the American Renaissance, pp. 369-386. Reprint of 1943.8.

Writings about Louisa May Alcott

1978

1. BAUM, FREDA L. "An Examination of Louisa May Alcott as 'New
    Woman.'" Unpublished thesis, Bowling Green State University,
    August.
    Examines Alcott's feminism with emphasis on the relation-
    ship between her feminism and her early abolitionist senti-
    ments. Examines in-depth magazine articles and the effect
    upon her female readers.

2. EASTON, BARBARA. "Feminism and the Contemporary Family."
    Socialist Review, 39 (May-June), 35n.
    Cites Little Women as nineteenth-century example containing
    patriarchal father, emotionally distant from mother and
    children.

1979

1. PAYNE, ALMA J. "Louisa May Alcott," in American Women Writers,
    A Critical Reference Guide. Vol. 1. New York: Frederick
    Ungar.
    Surveys Alcott's biography and assesses both Alcott's
    major works and selected critical treatments.

Index

Abbot, Willis, J., 1913.1
Abolition (Alcott and), 1929.6;
   1942.2; 1953.5; 1958.7;
   1970.1, 6; 1971.3
"About Little Women," 1903.2;
   1932.13
Across My Path, Memories of
   People I Have Known,
   1916.1; 1970.7
Adams, E. L., 1942.1
Adams, Mildred, 1865.3; 1938.1
Adelman, Joseph, 1926.1
Adlow, Dorothy, 1934.1
"Adventure with Little Women,
   An," 1915.1
Adventuring with Books, 1973.5
Ahlers, Lena C., 1932.1
Alcott, Amos Bronson, 1893.3;
   1902.1-2; 1908.1; 1909.2;
   1915.4; 1920.2; 1926.2, 6;
   1927.2; 1930.2; 1935.1-2;
   1938.6, 10, 12; 1970.2;
   1974.3
"Alcott Centenary," 1932.2
Alcott family, 1969.4
Alcott, May, 1934.1
Alcott Memoirs Posthumously
   Compiled from Papers, Jour-
   nals, and Memoranda of the
   Late Dr. Frederick L. H.
   Willis, 1915.2
Alcott myth, the, 1889.2;
   1929.2; 1938.6-8, 12-13;
   1947.2; 1960.2; 1964.1;
   1968.18, 20; 1970.7; 1971.1;
   1973.3; 1974.3; 1977.4
"Alcott's 'An Old-Fashioned
   Girl/A Collation,'" 1938.4

"Alcotts and Their Homes,"
   1902.1; 1968.4-5
Alcotts As I Knew Them, The,
   1909.2
Alcotts in Harvard, The, 1902.2
"Alcotts through Thirty Years,
   The: Letters to Alfred
   Whitman," 1957.7
All the Happy Endings, 1956.1
America in Fiction, 1967.4
American Authors, 1600-1900: A
   Biographical Dictionary of
   American Literature, 1938.9
American Authors, 1795-1895,
   1969.1
"American Children's Classics:
   Which Will Fade, Which Endure,"
   1972.1
American family in Alcott,
   1975.4-6, 8; 1976.4
"American First Editions,"
   1929.1
American Mind, The, 1950.2
American Novel, The, 1946.2
American Novel 1789-1959, The/A
   Checklist, 1961.2
American Pilgrimage, 1942.4;
   1943.4
Amos Bronson Alcott: His Life
   and Philosophy, 1893.3
"Analysis of the Playwriting
   Techniques of Clare Tree
   Major, An" 1977.3
Anonymous and pseudonymous works
   by Louisa May Alcott, 1877.1-
   4; 1943.1, 5, 8.
Anthony, Katharine S., 1936.3;
   1937.1; 1938.2-3, 5, 7-8, 11

Articles on American Literature, 1900-1950, 1954.3
Articles on American Literature, 1950-1967, 1970.5
Ashmun, M., 1907.1
Auerbach, Nina, 1976.4; 1977.1
Aunt Jo's Scrap Bag, 1872.1-2; 1873.1; 1874.1; 1879.1; 1929.4
"Austin and Alcott on Matriarchy: New Women or New Wives?," 1976.4
"Author," 1941.1
"Author of Little Women and Children's Books Today, The," 1932.7
Authors of Books for Young Children, 1971.7
"Authors vs. Critics: Children's Books in the 1870's," 1967.5
Ayer, Margaret (Illustrator), 1954.4

Bacon, E. M., 1902.1
Bannon, Barbara A., 1975.1
Barrett, C. Waller, 1957.2
Barrett, Wendell, 1901.1
Barsch, Frederica, ed., 1953.6
Baum, Freda L., 1978.1
Bazin, Henry, 1915.2
Beach, Seth Curtis, 1905.4; 1967.1
Becker, May Lamberton, 1933.2-3; 1936.1-2, 4-5
Bedell, Madelon, 1975.2
Beer, Thomas, 1926.2
Behind a Mask, 1975.1-2
Bibliographical sketches, 1901.1, 4; 1909.3; 1915.2, 4; 1926.5; 1927.1; 1931.3; 1932.4-6, 9, 12; 1938.4, 14; 1940.2; 1942.1; 1943.8; 1948.1; 1954.1, 3, 5; 1957.2; 1958.8; 1961.2; 1962.3; 1967.2, 5
Bibliographies, 1929.1; 1950.3-4; 1955.1; 1965.2; 1966.1, 3; 1969.5; 1970.3; 1971.2, 6; 1973.4

Biographical sketches, 1880.1; 1885.1-2; 1886.3; 1889.1; 1891.1-2; 1892.1; 1893.2; 1895.1; 1896.1; 1899.1; 1905.4; 1906.1-2; 1907.2; 1910.2; 1911.1-2; 1912.1-2; 1913.1; 1915.2, 4; 1916.1; 1917.1-2; 1919.3-4; 1922.2; 1923.1-2; 1924.1; 1925.1-2; 1926.3-6; 1927.2-3; 1928.1-2; 1932.1, 5, 8, 15; 1934.1; 1936.3, 6; 1937.1; 1938.9, 14; 1949.2; 1951.3; 1953.1; 1967.1; 1968.2-3, 14, 20; 1970.7; 1971.5
Biographies, 1888.2-3; 1889.2; 1909.3; 1914.1; 1932.10; 1936.4; 1938.3; 1942.4; 1950.3; 1954.4; 1958.12; 1977.4
Biographies and bibliographies, 1889.2; 1909.3; 1914.1; 1915.2; 1928.1; 1929.3; 1931.2; 1932.14
Blanck, Jacob N., 1938.4; 1940.2; 1943.1; 1955.1; 1965.2; 1967.2
Bliven, Bruce, 1964.1
Bolton, Sarah K., 1886.3; 1925.1; 1949.1; 1954.2
"Booklovers' Corner," 1933.8
"Books for Children," 1919.1
"Books that Separate Children from Their Parents," 1898.1, 3
Bonstelle, Jessie, 1914.1
Bradford, Gamaliel, 1919.3-4; 1933.4; 1968.2
Brazil, Angela, 1922.1
Bronson Alcott at Alcott House, England and Fruitlands, New England, 1908.1
Bronson Alcott's Fruitlands, 1915.4
Brooks, Van Wyck, 1950.1
Brophy, Brigid, 1964.2; 1965.3, 5; 1967.3
Brown, Mary Hosmer, 1926.3
Browning, David C., ed., 1962.1

Index

"Miss Alcott Speaking," 1957.1
"Miss Alcott's Stern Life
   Battle," 1889.1
Modern Mephistopheles, A,
   1877.1-4
"Money, the Job and Little
   Women," 1975.4
Montiero, George, 1976.8
Moods, 1865.1-3
Moore, Katharine, 1974.5
Moore, Rebecca Deming, 1923.1
Morris, Richard, ed., 1953.4
Morrow, Honoré Willsie, 1927.2
Morse, Katherine, 1926.4
Moses, Belle, 1909.3; 1931.1
Moss, Howard, 1974.6
"Most Beloved American Writer,"
   1937.1; 1938.3
"Mother of Little Women," 1938.11
Mother Was a Lady/Self and Soci-
   ety in Selected American
   Children's Periodicals, 1865-
   1890, 1970.4; 1974.4
"Mother Was a Lady; Strategy and
   Order in Selected American
   Children's Periodicals, 1865-
   1890," 1970.4; 1974.4
Mott, Frank Luther, 1947.1
Moulton, Louise Chandler, 1885.1

Nathan, George Jean, 1945.1;
   1946.1
"Negro Character in Northern
   Magazine Fiction of the
   1860's," 1970.1
Nesbitt, Elizabeth, 1953.3
New Champlin Encyclopaedia for
   Young Folks, The, 1924.1
New England Indian Summer,
   1950.1
"News from the Rare Book Sellers;
   Secret Literary Life,"
   1943.1
"News from the Rare Book Shops,"
   1940.2
"New Woman Revisited, The,"
   1974.2
Nisenson, Samuel, 1949.2
Northend, Mary H., 1923.2
Notable Women in History, 1913.1

"Not To Be Read on Sunday,"
   1968.20
"Novels of Louisa May Alcott as
   Commentary on the American
   Family, The," 1975.6

O'Faolain, Sean, 1968.18
Old-Fashioned Girl, An, 1870.1-9;
   1938.4
"On a Portrait of Miss Alcott"
   (Poem), 1907.1
Only Connect; Readings in Chil-
   dren's Literature, 1969.3
Oxford Companion to Literature,
   1948.2

Papashvily, Helen Waite, 1956.1;
   1965.1, 6-7
"Papers of Great Listed for
   Study," 1954.1
Parrington, Vernon, 1930.2
Parton, James, 1880.1; 1885.2
Part Taken by Women in American
   History, The, 1912.1
Pattee, Fred, 1915.3
Pauly, Thomas H., 1975.5
Payne, Alma J., 1973.3-4; 1979.1
Peare, Catherine O., 1954.4
Peattie, Donald, 1960.2
Peattie, Louise, 1960.2
Pedlar's Progress: The Life of
   Bronson Alcott, 1938.12
Perényi, Eleanor, 1955.2
"Philosopher and His Daughter,
   The: Amos Bronson Alcott and
   Louisa," 1974.3
Pickett, LaSalle (Corbell),
   1916.1; 1970.7
Pilgrim's Progress, 1968.14-15
Porter, Maria S., 1892.1; 1893.2
"Portrait," 1903.1
Portrait, 1932.13
"Portrait" (antislavery sympa-
   thizer), 1953.5
"Portrait of Louisa May Alcott,"
   1919.3
Portrait (Photograph), 1937.2
Portraits and Personalities,
   1933.4; 1968.2